READINGS IN ECONOMIC HISTORY
AND THEORY

Precursors of Adam Smith

Edited with an Introduction
and Notes by

RONALD L. MEEK

Tyler Professor of Economics
University of Leicester

Dent, London
Rowman and Littlefield, Totowa, N.J.

© J. M. Dent & Sons Ltd, 1973
All rights reserved
Made in Great Britain
at the
Aldine Press · Letchworth · Herts
for
J. M. DENT & SONS LTD
Aldine House · Albemarle Street · London
First published 1973

First published in the United States 1973 by
ROWMAN AND LITTLEFIELD
Totowa · New Jersey

Dent: ISBN 0 460 10195 1
Rowman and Littlefield: ISBN 0 87471 398 6

CONTENTS

INTRODUCTION

'Paradigms', wrote Professor T. S. Kuhn in his now-famous book on *The Structure of Scientific Revolutions*, are 'universally recognized scientific achievements that for a time provide model problems and solutions to a community of practitioners.'[1] Works like Aristotle's *Physica*, Newton's *Principia*, Franklin's *Electricity*, and Lavoisier's *Chemistry*, for example, 'served for a time implicitly to define the legitimate problems and methods of a research field for succeeding generations of practitioners'. They were able to do this, Professor Kuhn argues,

> because they shared two essential characteristics. Their achievement was sufficiently unprecedented to attract an enduring group of adherents away from competing modes of scientific activity. Simultaneously, it was sufficiently open-ended to leave all sorts of problems for the redefined group of practitioners to resolve.

From 'paradigms' sharing these two characteristics spring 'particular coherent traditions of scientific research'—those which 'the historian describes under such rubrics as "Ptolemaic astronomy" (or "Copernican"), "Aristotelian dynamics" (or "Newtonian"), "corpuscular optics" (or "wave optics"), and so on'.[2]

What about Smithian political economy, then? Professor Kuhn himself is reluctant to extend his concept of a paradigm from the natural to the social sciences;[3] but it can surely be claimed that Smith's *Wealth of Nations* (1776) possessed most of the basic characteristics of a paradigm as Professor Kuhn defines them. A 'group of adherents' was certainly attracted to its system from 'competing modes of scientific activity': its

---

[1] T. S. Kuhn, *The Structure of Scientific Revolutions* (2nd edn., 1970), p. viii.
[2] ibid., p. 10.
[3] 'It remains an open question what parts of social science have yet acquired such paradigms at all' (ibid., p. 15).

two main rivals—the system of the Physiocrats, and that of Steuart's *Inquiry*—did not long survive its publication. The group so attracted was certainly 'enduring': if we define the basic theoretical framework of the *Wealth of Nations* in reasonably broad terms, it can be argued that almost all major economists—including Ricardo, both Mills, and even in an important sense Marx—worked within it for nearly a century, if not longer. And the system of the *Wealth of Nations* was certainly 'open-ended' in Professor Kuhn's sense—i.e. it left many problems for later practitioners of the science to solve. It is true that a 'community of practitioners' in Professor Kuhn's sense could hardly be said to have existed in Smith's time (except perhaps in France), and that the significance of Smith's work extended far beyond the field of 'research' as Professor Kuhn implicitly defines it. But even if Smithian political economy cannot be described as a paradigm in the strict sense of the word, it surely represented one of the nearest approaches to it in the whole history of economic thought.

One of the crucial features of a change from one paradigm to another—i.e. a 'revolution'—in the natural sciences, according to Professor Kuhn, is a 'shift in scientific perception',[1] of such a character that 'objects that were grouped in the same set before are grouped in different ones afterward and vice versa'.[2] It was precisely a basic 'shift in perception' of this type which was the main achievement of the *Wealth of Nations*. As I see it, the really central element in that work was Smith's new division of society into landlords, wage-earners, and capitalists, which was implicitly accepted as a datum throughout and explicitly formulated in the following passage:

The whole annual produce of the land and labour of every country, or what comes to the same thing, the whole price of that annual produce, naturally divides itself, it has already been observed, into three parts; the rent of land, the wages of labour, and the profits of stock; and constitutes a revenue to three different orders of people; to those who live by rent, to those who live by wages, and to those who live by profit. These are the three great, original and constituent orders of every civilized society,

[1] ibid., p. 117.   [2] ibid., p. 200.

from whose revenue that of every other order is ultimately derived.[1]

Before Smith, the socio-economic structure had almost always been defined in terms of a pattern which either virtually ignored the existence of the third of these 'orders', or implicitly denied its 'great, original and constituent' character by including it in some other 'order'. Steuart's basic division, for example, was that between 'farmers' and 'free hands'; the French Physiocrats' was that between the landlords, the 'productive class' engaged in agriculture (which included both wage-earners and capitalists), and the 'sterile class' engaged in manufacture and trade (which consisted partly of wage-earners and capitalists, but mainly of workers on their own account). Comparing Smith's view with that of the Physiocrats, we see that whereas with the latter the capitalists were grouped in different sets, with Smith they came to be grouped in the same set. And this new way of looking at society made all the difference in the world.

First and foremost, it paved the way for the idea that the drive by the third 'constituent order' to maximize its profits and to accumulate capital was the mainspring of the mechanism of the economic process—the principal medium, in other words, through which the famous 'invisible hand' worked to improve human society. Over time, the drive to accumulate capital led to a substantial increase in real income;[2] and at any given time, the drive to maximize profits led to the optimum allocation of resources between different employments[3] and within each employment.[4] Second, and almost as important, it facilitated the formulation of certain key ideas about the *general* character of the modern 'commercial society' in which, as Smith put it, 'every man . . . lives by exchanging, or becomes in some measure a merchant'.[5] The point here was that the emergence of the capitalist class as a 'great, original and con-

[1] Smith, *Wealth of Nations* (ed. E. Cannan, 6th edn., 1950), Vol. I, p. 276.
[2] ibid., Vol. I, pp. 367.
[3] ibid., Vol. I, p. 475.
[4] ibid., Vol. I, p. 292.
[5] ibid., Vol. I, p. 26.

stituent order' had been associated historically with the dissolution of the old feudal ties and a considerable extension of the social division of labour, and had made it more and more difficult for any single individual to supply his own wants except by supplying those of others *in a particular way*—namely, by engaging in the production of commodities for the market. Thus the modern 'commercial society' could be plausibly visualized as one in which the chief tie between men was that which bound them together as producers of different commodities for the market.[1]

Smith's attitude towards the society whose outlines he thus delineated was essentially one of approval, and the policy he advocated in relation to it was essentially one of *laissez-faire*, even if both the approval and the policy were in certain respects qualified. But more important from the analytic viewpoint was the fact that his postulation of a society of this type, as he himself fairly clearly recognized, threw up a number of crucial problems for solution. The most basic problem—as it was bound to appear if one assumed as Smith did that the economy was ruled by the price mechanism—was that of *value*, in other words, roughly, the problem of what determined the prices of the goods and services which were bought and sold on the market. This problem was seen to be important not only in itself, but also because of the light which its solution could throw on the problem of the distribution of income, and, in particular, on the problem of the origin and level of capitalist profit. If the capitalists were in fact a genuinely 'independent' order, then the income which accrued to them must also be genuinely 'independent'. It could no longer be regarded, as most of the earlier economists had regarded it, as being 'derived from', or 'paid out of', or at any rate 'included in', the income of some other group; and its origin and level had to be explained in terms of the operation of the price mechanism. The solution to this problem, Smith believed, was the main key to the analysis of the whole process of production, distribution, and accumulation in a 'commercial society' which was predominantly capitalist and competitive in character.

But Smith's postulation of a society of this type not only

---

[1] cf. my *Studies in the Labour Theory of Value* 2nd edn., 1973, p. 38.

threw up these problems: it was also closely associated with certain basic elements of the general methodology which he employed in his endeavour to solve them. Three points are particularly important in this connection. First, if the economy as a whole was ruled by the price mechanism, then it could usefully be regarded as a kind of gigantic machine, operating through the buying and selling activities of individual economic agents to produce unintended but law-governed results, which were analysable (up to a point) with the aid of certain of the methods and concepts which had proved so successful in the natural sciences. Hence Smith's concept of what Schumpeter has called 'the universal interdependence of the magnitudes that constitute the economic cosmos';[1] hence, too, his use of the concept of equilibrium in his theory of value, in which the price of each commodity, under competitive conditions, is assumed to tend towards a 'natural' (i.e. equilibrium) level which just covers the rent, wages, and profits—each reckoned at its 'natural' rate—of the three 'constituent orders' participating in its production.

Second, if the tie which bound men to one another as producers of different commodities for the market had become of such paramount importance, then it seemed natural to conceive of the exchange of these commodities as being in essence the exchange of *quantities of social labour*—an idea which largely dictated the direction in which Smith (and Ricardo and Marx) looked for an explanation of what 'lay behind' or 'ultimately determined' the prices of commodities.

Third, i f the emergence to independence and power of the profit-receiving, labour-employing 'third order' was of such crucial significance, then it seemed appropriate to embody the new class relationships which had resulted from its emergence —in particular, the basic socio-economic relationship between the capitalists and the wage-earners whom they employed— as a kind of institutional datum in the model of the economic process. And for the same reason, it seemed appropriate at certain stages in the analysis, in order to highlight the distinctive features of the working of the economic machine under capitalism, to contrast this with its working in a simpler type of

---

[1] J. A. Schumpeter, *History of Economic Analysis* (1954), p. 308.

society from which the capitalist class had been, as it were, artificially abstracted.

I am not trying to claim, of course, that all these elements of Smith's system *arose out of* the basic 'shift in scientific perception' which I am talking about. There was scarcely a single element in Smith's system which was 'new' in the sense that Smith himself could clearly and unequivocally be said to have originated it. Even the vital concept of profit on capital as a new and independent category of class income, sharply differentiated from all other types of income—even, indeed, the basic 'shift in scientific perception' itself[1]—had to some extent been anticipated. All I am saying is that Smith made the 'shift' more decisively and consciously than even the most enlightened of his precursors, and in such a way that when he had made it all the other elements fell into place—and very often into a new place. Thus it seems to be very unhelpful to regard Smith, as some historians have done, as a mere synthesizer. Rather, as I have said, it is more appropriate to regard his system as a 'paradigm'—even if only in inverted commas—possessing a number of the leading characteristics of paradigms in the natural sciences. Professor Kuhn tells us that when natural scientists are led by a new paradigm, they 'see new and different things when looking with familiar instruments in places they have looked before. It is rather as if the professional community had been suddenly transported to another planet where familiar objects are seen in a different light and are joined by unfamiliar ones as well.'[2] This is not a bad description of what happened in the field of economics—albeit fairly gradually—after the publication of the *Wealth of Nations* in 1776.

If Smith's system was in fact a 'paradigm' in this sense, then, was it the *first* one in the history of economics? This is not entirely a question of semantics. As Professor Kuhn says, 'each of the schools whose competition characterizes the earlier [i.e. pre-paradigm] period is guided by something much like a

[1] I am thinking here mainly of Turgot's *Réflexions sur la Formation et la Distribution des Richesses*, which embodied a 'paradigm' very similar to Smith's. Turgot still maintained, however, that the profits of the capitalists were in a certain sense 'paid out of' the incomes of the proprietor and the agents of the 'productive class'. Profits were not, as it were, fully emancipated until the *Wealth of Nations*.

[2] Kuhn, op. cit., p. 111.

paradigm'.[1] And in the period before 1776 one of these competing schools in particular—that of the Physiocrats—was guided by something *so* much like a paradigm that if we apply the concept to Smith's system we can hardly refuse to apply it to theirs. Certainly, at any rate, the debate between Physiocratic and Smithian economists possessed one of the main characteristics which Professor Kuhn ascribes to debates between the proponents of competing paradigms in the natural sciences:

> The parties to such debates inevitably see differently certain of the experimental or observational situations to which both have recourse. Since the vocabularies in which they discuss such situations consist, however, predominantly of the same terms, they must be attaching some of these terms to nature differently, and their communication is inevitably only partial. As a result, the superiority of one theory to another is something that cannot be proved in the debate.[2]

When one thinks of the different meanings ascribed by Smith and the Physiocrats respectively to such terms as 'productive', 'profit', and 'net revenue', this has a very familiar ring. It should be added, however, that the situation in economics differs from that in the natural sciences in one very important respect—that the reality to which competing 'paradigms' refer is not necessarily quite the same reality, and not necessarily static, so that one 'paradigm' may win out over another—as Smith's did over that of the Physiocrats—largely because reality changes in such a way as to render the older one implausible. The Physiocratic notions that profit was derived from rent and that manufacture was 'sterile' could hardly have long survived the emergence to independence and power of the third 'constituent order' and the subordination of manufacture to the capitalist mode of production.

This general view of Smith's place in the history of economic thought has quite largely dictated my choice of the 'precursors' whose works are represented in this volume, and the particular extracts from these works which are reproduced. I have in-

---

[1] ibid., p. ix. [2] ibid., p. 198.

cluded, first, a number of pieces adumbrating certain important economic (and sociological) ideas which Smith later accepted, developed, and incorporated as individual elements in his system. But I have also included, second, a number containing 'paradigmatic' (or pseudo-'paradigmatic') ideas against which Smith reacted in order to form his own, competing, 'paradigm'. Thus besides certain key passages from the work of men like Hutcheson and Hume which most people would expect to find in a book of readings with the title *Precursors of Adam Smith*, I have included a number of pieces by Physiocratic writers whom one might not have expected to be given quite such prominence. Had I been primarily interested in other aspects of Smith's system, of course, my selection might have been quite different. This collection of readings, then, is based on a view of the *Wealth of Nations* which may not be shared by all historians—but it will not, I hope, be regarded for this reason as any the less interesting.

Because of the obvious constraint of space, and in order to prevent the extracts becoming too 'bitty', I have confined myself, with one exception, to works published during the period from 1750 to 1775, the quarter-century that immediately preceded the appearance of the *Wealth of Nations*.[1] The exception is Turgot's unfinished essay on *Value and Money*, which although written during the period concerned was not discovered and published until much later. I have also confined myself—with the same exception—to works with which we may fairly safely assume that Smith himself was familiar.[2]

[1] The works by Cantillon and Hutcheson, although published during the period in question, were actually written much earlier.
[2] Of the seven remaining works, those by Cantillon, Hutcheson, Hume, and Steuart, and the *Philosophie Rurale* by Mirabeau and Quesnay, were all in Smith's library. So far as Mirabeau's *L'Ami des Hommes* is concerned, we know that Smith's library contained five volumes of this work, but we do not know whether these included the particular volume containing the *Tableau Oeconomique avec ses Explications*. This does not really matter, however, since Smith's references to the *Tableau* in the *Wealth of Nations* show that he was quite familiar with it in several of its formulations. So far as Tucker is concerned, the particular essay from which our extract is taken does not seem to have been in Smith's library, but several other works by Tucker were, and it would seem very unlikely that Smith was unacquainted with the essay in question.

INTRODUCTION

On the title page to each set of extracts I have put a note concerning sources, omissions, footnotes,[1] etc.; and each set is preceded by a short introduction usually containing a biographical note, an account of the origin of the work concerned, a guide to and explanation of some of the key ideas in the extracts, and a note of some of their links with the *Wealth of Nations*.

R. L. M.

University of Leicester, 1973

---

[1] All footnotes keyed in by numerical indicators are mine, and all those keyed in by any other method are those of the author concerned.

SELECT BIBLIOGRAPHY

GENERAL

E. A. J. Johnson, *Predecessors of Adam Smith* (1937)
T. S. Kuhn, *The Structure of Scientific Revolutions* (2nd edn., 1970)
R. L. Meek, *Economics and Ideology* (1967)
A. E. Monroe (ed.), *Early Economic Thought* (1945)
J. A. Schumpeter, *History of Economic Analysis* (1954)
Hannah R. Sewell, *The Theory of Value before Adam Smith* (1901)
J. J. Spengler and W. R. Allen (eds.), *Essays in Economic Thought: Aristotle to Marshall* (1960)
G. S. L. Tucker, *Progress and Profits in British Economic Thought, 1650–1850* (1960)

ADAM SMITH

J. Hollander (ed.), *Adam Smith, 1776–1926* (1928)
J. Rae, *Life of Adam Smith* (1895)
W. R. Scott, *Adam Smith as Student and Professor* (1937)
A. Skinner, Introduction to the Pelican edition of Smith's *Wealth of Nations* (1970)

RICHARD CANTILLON

H. Higgs, 'Life and Work of Richard Cantillon', in the Royal Economic Society's edition of Cantillon's *Essai sur la Nature du Commerce en Général* (1931)
W. S. Jevons, 'Richard Cantillon and the Nationality of Political Economy', reprinted in the above edition.
J. J. Spengler, 'Richard Cantillon: First of the Moderns', reprinted in J. J. Spengler and W. R. Allen (eds.), op. cit.

FRANCIS HUTCHESON

W. R. Scott, *Francis Hutcheson* (1900)
W. L. Taylor, *Francis Hutcheson and David Hume as Predecessors of Adam Smith* (1965)

SELECT BIBLIOGRAPHY

DAVID HUME

M. Arkin, 'The Economic Writings of David Hume—A Reassessment', reprinted in J. J. Spengler and W. R. Allen (eds.), op. cit.

E. Rotwein, Introduction to *David Hume: Writings on Economics* (1955)

W. L. Taylor, *Francis Hutcheson and David Hume as Predecessors of Adam Smith* (1965)

A. R. J. TURGOT

D. Dakin, *Turgot and the Ancien Régime* (1939)

P. D. Groenewegen, 'Turgot and Adam Smith' (*Scottish Journal of Political Economy*, Vol. XVI)

R. L. Meek, *Turgot on Progress, Sociology and Economics* (1973)

THE FRENCH PHYSIOCRATS

H. Higgs, *The Physiocrats* (1897)

R. L. Meek, *The Economics of Physiocracy* (1962)

J. J. Spengler, 'The Physiocrats and Say's Law of Markets', reprinted in J. J. Spengler and W. R. Allen (eds.), op. cit.

SIR JAMES STEUART

S. R. Sen, *The Economics of Sir James Steuart* (1957)

A. Skinner, Introduction to the Scottish Economic Society's edition of Steuart's *An Inquiry into the Principles of Political Oeconomy* (1966)

JOSIAH TUCKER

R. L. Schuyler (ed.), *Josiah Tucker: A Selection from his Economic and Political Writings* (1931)

Richard Cantillon

FOUR CHAPTERS FROM

ESSAY ON THE NATURE OF TRADE IN GENERAL

(1755)

Source: The four chapters have been newly translated from pp. 26–56 of the French text of the *Essay* as reproduced in the edition published (with an English translation) in 1931 under the editorship of Henry Higgs. There are no omissions. The new translation, although it follows Higgs's in some places, departs from it quite appreciably in others. All the footnotes are the present editor's.

Richard Cantillon (1680?–1734) was a Paris banker of Irish extraction, who wrote his famous *Essai sur la Nature du Commerce en Général* round about 1730. This work, although not published in the formal sense until 1755, apparently achieved a limited circulation before that date in manuscript form, and exercised a considerable influence on Turgot (via Gournay), Quesnay, and Mirabeau. The extent of Cantillon's direct influence on Adam Smith is debatable, but it is perhaps noteworthy that Cantillon is one of the relatively few previous authors whom Smith quotes by name in the *Wealth of Nations*.[1]

In the first nine chapters of the *Essai*, preceding the four included in our extracts, Cantillon begins by presenting a brief historical-cum-sociological analysis of the class structure of society. In the leading position, historically and analytically, stand the proprietors of land, whose estates are cultivated by farmers [*fermiers*] and/or husbandmen [*laboureurs*]. As society develops, and villages, towns, and cities are established, certain other classes—'artisans', 'merchants', and 'entrepreneurs', etc.—come into existence in order to meet the needs of the three agricultural classes, and, of course, the needs of one another. This kind of approach to economic analysis, via history and sociology, was destined to become of increasing importance as the eighteenth century progressed.

After three chapters in which he deals with differences in remuneration as between husbandmen and artisans and as between artisans in different trades, and with the way in which the number of members of these groups in a state is 'naturally proportioned' to the demand for their services, Cantillon comes on to the analysis of value which is the main subject of Chapters X and XI (below, pp. 5–13). Here he begins by making a key distinction between the market price of a commodity and what he calls its 'intrinsic value', the latter being 'the measure of the quantity of land and labour which enters into its production,

[1] *Wealth of Nations* (ed. E. Cannan, 6th edn., 1950), Vol. I, p. 76.

having regard to the fertility or product of the land and to the quality of the labour' (p. 7). He then proceeds to argue that at any rate in 'well-ordered societies', and at any rate in the case of commodities 'whose consumption is fairly constant and uniform', the market prices of these commodities 'do not deviate much from the intrinsic value' (below, p. 8). We see here the beginnings of the Classical idea, developed in particular by Smith, that in a competitive situation the forces of demand and supply will tend to fix prices at a 'natural' or equilibrium level which is not arbitrary, but determined by the 'cost of production' (in some sense or other) of the commodity. But Cantillon says little in the *Essai* about the mechanism by which the market price is *made* equal to the 'intrinsic value'; and there is not much more than an inkling here and there of the Smithian notion of profit on capital as an independent constituent of the 'natural price'. The passage about the hatters on p. 18 below represents one of Cantillon's nearest approaches to the Classical viewpoint on these issues.

In Chapter XI (below, pp. 8–13), Cantillon deals with the vexing problem of what Sir William Petty had called the 'par' between land and labour. Looking at his discussion from the point of view of later Classical developments in value theory, we can say, perhaps, that what he was trying to do was to 'reduce' one of these two elements to the other so as to transform what would otherwise be a dualistic theory of value into a monistic one. His solution, which involves the 'reduction' of labour to land rather than *vice versa*, is extremely ingenious, if not entirely convincing; and the 'sociological' elements in his account are particularly interesting.

Chapter XIII (below, pp. 16–21), perhaps the most remarkable chapter in the whole book, is devoted more or less exclusively to 'entrepreneurs'. Here Cantillon makes a clear distinction between 'entrepreneurs' and 'people on wages' (p. 19), and lays a startlingly modern emphasis on the risk-bearing aspect of entrepreneurship. With Cantillon, however, the entrepreneurial class includes not only capitalists, but also those who are 'entrepreneurs of their own labour without any capital' (p. 19)—chimney-sweeps, needlewomen, water-carriers, and even beggars and robbers; and the 'profit' which members of this very broad class receive seems usually to be regarded as a

4

kind of superior and indeterminate wage rather than as an income related to the amount of capital employed.[1] Cantillon is in effect postulating the existence of a society in which the capitalist entrepreneur is only just beginning to separate himself out from the ranks of the workers on their own account. The 'paradigms' generated in a society of this type are bound to be essentially different from those generated in a society where it is assumed that the process of separation has been completed.

In Cantillon's society, the other side of this coin is the predominant position of the proprietors of land, at whose expense all the other orders are assumed—for reasons set out, not very clearly, in Chapter XII (below, pp. 14–16)—to subsist or be enriched. This notion of the predominance of the proprietors is closely associated with and largely supported by the notion of a circular flow of income between the different social groups; and it seems probable that this part of Cantillon's analysis had a considerable influence on Quesnay, in whose system the two notions are juxtaposed and associated in a very similar manner. The passages on pp. 14–15 below read very much like a first sketch, in words rather than figures, of the *Tableau Économique*.

ESSAY ON THE NATURE OF TRADE IN GENERAL

Part One, Chapter X

The price and intrinsic value of a thing in general is the measure of the land and labour which enter into its production

One acre of land produces more wheat, or feeds more sheep, than another acre; the labour of one man is dearer than that of another man, depending upon the art concerned and the cir-

---

[1] In Part Two, Chapter ix, however, where he treats 'Of the interest of money, and of its causes', Cantillon comes a little closer to the Classical concept than he does in the extracts reproduced in the present volume.

cumstances, as has already been explained.[1] If two acres of land are of the same fertility, one acre will maintain as many sheep and produce the same quantity of wool as the other, assuming the labour to be the same; and the wool produced by the one will be sold at the same price as that produced by the other.

If wool is made on the one hand into a coat of coarse cloth, and on the other hand into a coat of fine cloth, since the latter coat will require more labour and dearer labour than the coat of coarse cloth, it will sometimes be ten times dearer, although both coats contain the same quantity of wool of the same quality. The quantity of the product of the land, and the quantity as well as the quality of the labour, will necessarily enter into the price.

A pound of flax made into fine Brussels lace requires the labour of fourteen persons for a year or the labour of one person for fourteen years, as may be seen from a calculation of the different parts of the operation in the Supplement,[2] where we also see that the price which is given for this lace suffices to pay for the maintenance of one person for fourteen years, and also to pay the profits of all the entrepreneurs and merchants concerned.

The fine steel spring which regulates an English watch is normally sold at a price which makes the proportion of the material to the labour, or of the steel to the spring, as one to 1,538,460,[3] so that the labour here makes up almost the whole value of the spring. See the calculation in the Supplement.

On the other hand, the price of the hay in a meadow, paid on the spot, or of a wood which it is proposed to cut down, is regulated by the material, or by the product of the land, according to its fertility.

The price of a jug of water from the river Seine is zero, because here we have a huge amount of material which never dries up; but in the streets of Paris people give a sou for it,

[1] Mainly in Chapters vii and viii, not included in these extracts.
[2] The Supplement mentioned here and elsewhere by Cantillon has been lost.
[3] The original has 'one to one', which is obviously an error. The figure 1,538,460 is that which appears at the relevant place in the manuscript version of the *Essay* which Mirabeau possessed and upon which he wrote extensive comments.

which is the price or measure of the labour of the water-carrier.

From these inductions and examples, I think it will be understood that the price or intrinsic value of a thing is the measure of the quantity of land and labour which enters into its production, having regard to the fertility or product of the land and to the quality of the labour.

But it often happens that a number of things which currently have this intrinsic value are not sold on the market in accordance with this value: that will depend on the humours and fancies of men, and on their consumption.

If a nobleman cuts canals and erects terraces in his garden, their intrinsic value will be proportionate to the land and labour; but the price in actual fact will not always follow this proportion: if he offers to sell this garden, it may happen that no one will be willing to give him half the expense he has incurred; and it may also happen, if a number of persons have a fancy for it, that he will be given double its intrinsic value, that is, double the value of the land[1] and the expense he has incurred.

If the farmers in a state sow more wheat than usual, that is, much more wheat than is needed for the year's consumption, the real and intrinsic value of the wheat will correspond to the land and labour which enter into its production: but as there is too great an abundance of it, and more sellers than buyers, the price of wheat on the market will necessarily fall below the intrinsic price or value. If on the other hand the farmers sow less wheat than is needed for consumption, there will be more buyers than sellers, and the price of wheat on the market will rise above its intrinsic value.

There is never any variation in the intrinsic value of things; but the impossibility of proportioning the production of commodities and produce to their consumption in a state causes a daily variation and a perpetual ebb and flow in market prices.

---

[1] *Fond*, corresponding in modern French to *fonds*. This word, which Cantillon uses very frequently, is difficult to translate because of its multiple meanings: it may mean (as here) land, or a landed estate; funds, or capital; means, or resources; stocks, or securities; or some combination of these notions. I have used the nearest English single-word equivalent, varying with the context, but have put *fond* or *fonds* in square brackets after it in cases where the word I have used may not fully reflect the meaning which seems to be implied in the text.

Nevertheless, in well-ordered societies the market prices of produce and commodities whose consumption is fairly constant and uniform do not deviate much from the intrinsic value; and except in years of too much scarcity or too much abundance the city magistrates are always able to fix the market price of many things, such as bread and meat, without anyone having cause to complain.

Land is the material, and labour is the form, of all produce and commodities; and since those who labour must necessarily subsist on the product of land, it would seem that a relation might be found between the value of labour and that of the product of land. This will be the subject of the next chapter.

Part One, Chapter XI

Of the par or relation between the value of land and the value of labour

It does not appear that Providence has given the right of possession of land to one man rather than to another. The most ancient titles are founded on violence and conquest. The lands of Mexico belong today to the Spaniards, and those of Jerusalem to the Turks. But in whatever way the ownership and possession of land are acquired, we have already observed[1] that it always falls into the hands of a small number of people in relation to the total inhabitants.

If the proprietor of a large estate undertakes to turn it to account himself, he will employ slaves, or free men, in order to work on it. If he employs a number of slaves, he must have overseers to keep them at work; he must also have artisan slaves to supply all the conveniences and pleasures of life for himself and for those whom he employs; and he must have trades taught to others in order that the work may be continued.

In this type of economy, he must give his slaves who are husbandmen an ordinary subsistence and the means to bring up their children. He must give their overseers benefits proportionate to the confidence and authority which they possess;

---

[1] In Chapter ii, not included in these extracts.

8

he must maintain the slaves to whom he has trades taught during the period of their apprenticeship without any return; and he must accord to the artisan slaves who are at work, and to their overseers, who must be well versed in the trades, a subsistence which is proportionately greater than that of the slaves who are husbandmen, etc., since the loss of an artisan would be more important than that of a husbandman, and since more care ought to be taken of him, in view of the fact that it always costs something to have a trade taught to the one who takes his place.

On this assumption, the labour of the lowest adult slave is worth at least as much as, and corresponds to, the quantity of land which the proprietor is obliged to employ for his food and necessary conveniences, and also to double the quantity of land which is necessary to bring up a child to working age, seeing that one-half of the children who are born die before the age of seventeen, according to the calculations and observations of the celebrated Dr Halley.[1] Thus two children must be brought up in order to keep one of working age, and it would seem that even on this basis enough would not be supplied to ensure a continuation of the work, because adult men die at all ages.

It is true that the one-half of the children who are born and who die before the age of seventeen die much faster in the first years of their life than in the following years, since a good third of those who are born die in their first year. This circumstance would seem to lower the cost required to bring up a child to working age: but since the mothers lose a great deal of time in taking care of their children in illness and infancy, and since the daughters even when grown up are not the equals of males in work and barely earn their subsistence, it seems that in order to keep one of two children who are brought up to manhood or to working age, as much of the product of land must be employed as for the subsistence of an adult slave, whether the proprietor brings up these children himself in his house or has them brought up there, *or whether the slave father brings them up in a house or hamlet apart. Thus I conclude that the daily labour of the lowest slave corresponds in value to double the product of the land on which he subsists, whether the proprietor*

[1] The reference is to Edward Halley's *Tables of Mortality from Observations made at Breslau* (1692).

gives it to him for his own subsistence and that of his family, or whether he has him and his family provided with subsistence in his own house. This is a matter which does not admit of exact calculation and in which precision is indeed not very necessary; it suffices that one does not deviate a great deal from reality.

If the proprietor employs vassals or free peasants in his work, he will probably maintain them at a rather higher standard than he would slaves, according to the custom of the locality; but even on this assumption the labour of the free husbandman ought to correspond in value to double the product of land needed for his maintenance. But it would always be more beneficial to the proprietor to keep slaves rather than free peasants, in view of the fact that when he has brought up too great a number of them for his work he can sell the surplus as he does his live-stock and obtain a price for them proportionate to the cost he has incurred in bringing them up to manhood or to working age, except in cases of old age or infirmity.

In the same way we may estimate the labour of artisan slaves at double the product of land which they consume; and that of the overseers of labour likewise, with allowance for the favours and benefits given to them above those who work under their direction.

If they are married, the husbandmen or artisans, when they have their double portion at their own disposition, employ one portion for their own maintenance, and the other for that of their children.

If they are unmarried, they will set aside a small part of their double portion to put themselves in a position to marry and to establish a small fund [*fond*] for the household; but most of them will consume the double portion for their own maintenance.

For example, the married peasant will content himself with living on bread, cheese, vegetables, etc., will rarely eat meat, will drink little wine or beer, and will have scarcely any but old and shabby clothes, which he will wear as long as he can: he will employ the surplus of his double portion in bringing up and maintaining his children; whereas the unmarried peasant will eat meat as often as he can, will provide himself with new clothes, etc., and consequently will employ his double portion for his own maintenance. Thus he will consume twice as much of the product of land for his personal needs as will the married peasant.

I do not take account here of the expense of the wife. I assume that her labour is barely sufficient to provide for her own maintenance, and when a large number of small children are to be seen in one of these poor households, I assume that some charitable persons contribute something towards their subsistence, without which the husband and wife must deprive themselves of a part of their necessaries in order to enable their children to live.

To understand this better, we should be aware of the fact that a poor peasant can maintain himself, at the lowest computation, on the product of an acre and a half of land, if he lives on bread and vegetables, and wears hempen clothes and wooden shoes, etc., whereas if he can allow himself wine and meat, woollen clothes, etc., he will be able without drunkenness or gluttony or any excess to expend the product of four to ten acres of land of average fertility, such as is most of the land in Europe taking one part with another. I have had some calculations made, which will be found in the Supplement, to determine the quantity of land the product of which one man may consume in a year in the form of each kind of food, clothing, and other things necessary for life, according to the modes of life in Europe today, where the peasants of different countries are often fed and maintained at quite different levels.

It was for this reason that I did not lay down how much land the labour of the lowest peasant or husbandman corresponds to in value, when I stated that it is worth double the product of the land which serves to maintain him, for this varies according to the mode of life in different countries. In some southern provinces of France, the peasant maintains himself on the product of an acre and a half of land, and his labour may there be estimated as equal to the product of three acres. But in the County of Middlesex, the peasant normally expends the product of five to eight acres of land, and one may therefore estimate his labour at double this.

In the country of the Iroquois, where the inhabitants do not cultivate the land, and where they live entirely by hunting, the lowest hunter may consume the product of fifty acres of land, since it probably requires this number of acres to feed the animals he eats in a year, more especially as these savages are not industrious enough to grow grass by cutting down a few trees, but leave everything to the will of nature.

Thus we may estimate the labour of this hunter as equal in value to the product of a hundred acres of land. In the southern provinces of China, the land produces up to three crops of rice in a year, and yields each time up to a hundred times the amount sown, thanks to the great attention which is paid to agriculture there, and to the fertility of the land, which is never allowed to lie fallow. The peasants, who work on it almost completely naked, live only on rice and drink nothing but rice-water, and it would appear that one acre maintains more than ten peasants: it is not surprising, therefore, that the population is prodigiously large there. However this may be, it would seem from these examples that it is a matter of complete indifference to nature whether the land produces grass, wood, or grain, or maintains a large or small number of plants, animals, or men.

The farmers in Europe seem to correspond to the overseers of slave husbandmen in other countries, and the master artisans who put several journeymen to work to the overseers of slave artisans.

These master artisans know roughly how much work a journeyman artisan can do in a day in each trade, and often pay them in proportion to the work they do; thus these journeymen, in their own interest, work as hard as they can without any other superintendence.

Since the farmers and master artisans in Europe are all entrepreneurs working at a risk, some get rich and earn more than a double subsistence, while others are ruined and become bankrupt, as will be explained in more detail when we deal with entrepreneurs;[1] but the majority maintain themselves and their families from day to day, and their labour or superintendence may be estimated at about three times the product of land which serves for their maintenance.

It is certain that these farmers and master artisans, if they direct the labour of ten husbandmen or journeymen, would be equally capable of directing the labour of twenty, according to

[1] See Chapter xiii below, pp. 16–21.

the size of their farms or the number of their customers, and this renders uncertain the value of their labour or superintendence.

From these inductions, and others which could be made in the same manner, we see that the value of a day's labour has a relation to the product of the land, and that the intrinsic value of a thing may be measured by the quantity of land which is employed in its production, and by the quantity of labour which enters into it, in other words by the quantity of land whose product is assigned to those who have worked on it; and since all this land belongs to the prince and to the proprietors, all things which have this intrinsic value have it only at their expense.

Money or silver, which finds in exchange the proportions of values, is the most certain measure for judging of the par between land and labour, and the relation which one has to the other in the different countries where this par varies according to the greater or smaller amount of the product of land which is assigned to those who labour.

For example, if one man earns an ounce of silver every day by his labour, and another in the same place earns only half an ounce, it may be concluded that the first has as much again of the product of land to expend as the second.

Sir William Petty, in a little manuscript of 1685,[1] regards this par or equation of land and labour as the most important consideration in political arithmetic; but the research which he has carried out into it in passing is merely fanciful and remote from natural laws, because he has fastened not on causes and principles but only on effects, as Mr Locke and Mr Davenant, and all the other English authors who have written anything on this subject, have done after him.

---

[1] The reference is probably to Petty's *Political Anatomy of Ireland*, which was published in 1691.

Part One, Chapter XII

All the orders and all the men in a state subsist or are enriched at the expense of the proprietors of land

It is only the prince and the proprietors of land who live in independence; all the other orders and all the inhabitants are in someone's pay or are entrepreneurs. The induction and details of this will be dealt with at greater length in the following chapter.

If the prince and the proprietors of land were to close down their estates, and were unwilling to allow anyone to cultivate them, it is obvious that there would be neither food nor clothing for any of the inhabitants of the state; consequently all the inhabitants of the state subsist not only on the product of the land which is cultivated on the proprietor's account, but also at the expense of these same proprietors from whose land [*fond*] they derive everything that they have.

The farmers normally have two-thirds of the product of the land, one-third for their costs and the maintenance of their assistants, and one-third for the profit of their enterprise. From these two-thirds the farmer generally provides subsistence, directly or indirectly, for all those who live in the countryside, and also for numbers of artisans or entrepreneurs in the city, through the commodities from the city which are consumed in the countryside.

The proprietor normally has one-third of the product of his land, and from this one-third he provides subsistence not only for all the artisans and others whom he employs in the city, but also, very frequently, for the carriers who bring the produce of the countryside to the city.

It is generally assumed that half of the inhabitants of a state subsist and make their abode in the cities, and the other half in the countryside. On this supposition, the farmer who has two-thirds or four-sixths of the product of the land, gives one-sixth of it directly or indirectly to the inhabitants of the city in exchange for the commodities which he gets from them. This one-sixth, together with the one-third or two-sixths which the proprietor spends in the city, makes up three-sixths or one-half of the product of the land. This calculation is only meant to give a general idea of the proportion; for after all, if half of the inhabitants live in the city, they spend more than half of the product of the land, considering that the inhabitants of the city live better than those of the countryside, and spend more of the product of the land, being all artisans or dependents of the proprietors and consequently maintained at a higher level than the assistants and dependents of the farmers.

However this may be, if we examine the means from which an inhabitant is supported, we will always find when we go back to their source that they arise from the land of the proprietor, either in the two-thirds of the product which is assigned to the farmer, or in the one-third which remains to the proprietor.

If a proprietor had only the amount of land which he lets out to a single farmer, this farmer would get a better living out of it than the proprietor himself; but the noblemen and proprietors of large estates in the cities sometimes have several hundred farmers, and are themselves very few in number in relation to all the inhabitants of a state.

It is true that in large cities there are often numbers of entrepreneurs and artisans who get their living from foreign trade, and therefore at the expense of the proprietors of land in foreign countries: but at the moment I am considering a state only in relation to its own product and its own industry, in order not to complicate my argument with accidental circumstances.

The landed estates belong to the proprietors, but these estates would become useless to them if they were not cultivated. The more they are worked, all other things being equal, the more produce they yield; and the more this produce is worked up, all other things being equal, the more value it has when it is made into commodities. This means that the proprietors have need for the other inhabitants, just as the latter have need of the proprietors; but in this type of economy it is for the proprietors, who have the disposition and direction of the land [*fonds*], to give the most advantageous turn and movement to the whole. Also, everything in a state depends principally upon the fancies and modes and fashions of life, of the proprietors of land, as I shall try to make clear later in this essay.[1]

It is need and necessity which enable farmers and artisans of all kinds, merchants, officers, soldiers and sailors, servants, and all the other orders who work or are employed in the state, to subsist there. All these working people not only serve the prince and the proprietors, but also reciprocally serve one another, so that there are numbers of them who do not work directly for the proprietors of land, and it is therefore not perceived that they are supported by the land of these proprietors, and that they live at their expense. As for those who carry on occupations which are not essential, like dancers, actors, painters, musicians, etc., they are maintained in the state only for pleasure or ornament, and their number is always very small in relation to the other inhabitants.

Part One, Chapter XIII

The circulation and exchange of produce and commodities, as well as their production, are carried on in Europe by entrepreneurs, and at a risk

The farmer is an entrepreneur who promises to pay to the proprietor, for his farm or land, a fixed sum of money (generally assumed to be equal in value to one-third of the product of the land), without any certainty of the benefit which he will derive from this enterprise. He employs a part of this land to feed flocks, to produce corn, wine, hay, etc., according to his fancy, without being able to foresee which of these kinds of produce will fetch the best price. The price of this produce will depend in part on the season and in part on the consumption; if wheat is abundant relatively to consumption, it will be dirt cheap; if it is scarce, it will be dear. Who can foresee the number of births and deaths among the inhabitants of the state in the course of a year? Who can foresee the increase or reduction of family expenditure which may occur? Yet the price of the farmer's produce naturally depends upon these circumstances which he

---

[1] In Chapters xiv and xv, not included in these extracts.

cannot foresee, and consequently he conducts the enterprise of his farm under uncertainty.

The city consumes more than half the produce of the farmer. He carries it to market there, or sells it in the market of the nearest small town, or else some individuals set up as entrepreneurs in order to carry on this transport. These bind themselves to pay the farmer a certain price for his produce, which will be the market price of the day, in order to obtain for it in the city an uncertain price, which ought however to defray the costs of carriage and leave them a profit for their enterprise. But the daily variation in the price of produce in the city, although not very great, renders their profit uncertain.

The entrepreneur or merchant who transports the produce of the countryside to the city cannot remain there to sell it retail as it is consumed. No city family will burden itself with buying at one and the same time all the produce which it would be capable of consuming, each family being liable to increase or decrease in size as well as in the level of its consumption, or at least to alter the kinds of produce which it will consume. Virtually the only product kept in stock by families is wine. However this may be, the majority of the inhabitants of the city, who only live from day to day but who are nevertheless the largest consumers, are unable to lay in any stocks of the produce of the countryside.

This means that numbers of people in the city set up as merchants or entrepreneurs in order to buy the produce of the countryside from those who bring it, or to have it brought on their account. They give a certain price for it according to that of the place where they buy it, in order to resell it wholesale or retail at an uncertain price.

Such entrepreneurs are the wholesale merchants in wool and corn, the bakers, butchers, manufacturers, and all the merchants of every kind who buy the produce and materials of the countryside, in order to work them up and resell them as the inhabitants need them for their consumption.

These entrepreneurs can never know the level of consumption in their city, nor even how long their purchasers will buy of them, since their rivals will try by all sorts of means to attract customers away from them. All this causes so much uncertainty among all these entrepreneurs that every day we see some of them go bankrupt.

The manufacturer who has bought wool from the merchant or direct from the farmer cannot know the profit he will make from his enterprise in selling his cloths and materials to the merchant clothier. If there is not an adequate demand for the latter's products, he will not burden himself with the cloths and materials of the manufacturer, especially if these materials cease to be in fashion.

The clothier is an entrepreneur who buys the cloths and materials of the manufacturer at a certain price in order to resell them at an uncertain price, because he cannot foresee the level of consumption. It is true that he can fix a price and stubbornly refrain from selling unless he obtains it; but if his customers leave him in order to buy more cheaply from someone else, he will be devoured by expenses while he is waiting to sell at the price he has in view, and this will ruin him just as effectively, or more effectively, than if he sold without any profit.

Shopkeepers, and retailers of all kinds, are entrepreneurs who buy at a certain price and who resell in their shops or in the market-places at an uncertain price. What encourages and maintains these kinds of entrepreneurs in a state is the fact that the consumers who are their customers prefer paying a little more to find what they need ready to hand in small quantities rather than laying in a stock of it, and that the majority of them do not have the means to lay in a stock of this kind by buying at first hand.

All these entrepreneurs become reciprocally consumers and customers of one another: the clothier of the wine merchant, and the latter of the clothier. They proportion themselves in the state to their customers or to their consumption. If there are too many hatters in a city or in a street for the number of people who buy hats there, some who are least patronized must go bankrupt; whereas if there are too few, it will be a profitable enterprise, which will encourage some new hatters to open shops there; and it is in this way that entrepreneurs of all kinds proportion themselves at a risk in a state.

All the other entrepreneurs, such as those who take charge of mines, entertainments, buildings, etc., merchants by sea and by land, etc., cook-shop proprietors, pastry-cooks, inn-keepers, etc., as well as entrepreneurs of their own labour who need no capital [*fonds*] to establish themselves, such as journeyman artisans, coppersmiths, needlewomen, chimney-sweeps, and water-carriers, live under uncertainty, and proportion themselves to their customers. Master artisans, such as shoemakers, tailors, joiners, wig-makers, etc., who employ journeymen in proportion to the work they have, live under the same uncertainty, since their customers may leave them from one day to another: the entrepreneurs of their own labour in the arts and sciences, such as painters, doctors, barristers, etc., live under the same uncertainty. If one attorney or barrister earns 5000 pounds sterling per year in the service of his clients or customers, and another earns only 500, they may be considered as having so much uncertain wages from those who employ them.

It may perhaps be suggested that all entrepreneurs try to grab everything they can in their calling, and to dupe their customers, but this is outside my subject.

On the basis of all these inductions, and a host of others which could be made in a topic which has for its object all the inhabitants of a state, it may be laid down that, except for the prince and the proprietors of land, all the inhabitants of a state are dependent; that they may be divided into two classes, namely entrepreneurs and people on wages; and that the entrepreneurs are as it were on uncertain wages, and all the others on certain wages for the period during which they receive them, even though their functions and ranks may be very unequal. The general with his pay, the courtier with his pension, and the servant with his wages, all fall into the latter category. All the others are entrepreneurs, whether they establish themselves with a capital [*fond*] in order to conduct their enterprise, or whether they are entrepreneurs of their own labour without any capital, and they may be considered as living under uncertainty; beggars even, and robbers, are entrepreneurs of this class. Finally, all the inhabitants of a state derive their subsistence and their benefits from the property [*fond*] of the proprietors of land, and are dependent.

It is nevertheless true that if some inhabitant on high wages, or some well-to-do entrepreneur, has saved goods or wealth,

19

that is, if he has stores of corn, wool, copper, gold or silver, or some type of produce or commodity which is constantly used or sold in a state and which has an intrinsic or real value, he may justly be considered independent to the extent of this capital [*fond*]. He may dispose of it to acquire a mortgage, and an income from land, and from stock [*fonds*] issued by the state when it borrows on the security of land: he may even live much better than the proprietors of small estates, and may even buy the property of some of them.

But produce and commodities, even gold and silver, are much more subject to accident and loss than the ownership of land; and in whatever way one may have gained or saved them, they are always derived from the land [*fond*] of the existing proprietors, either through gain, or through saving from the wages destined for one's subsistence.

The number of proprietors of money in a large state is often fairly considerable; and although the value of all the money which circulates in the state barely exceeds a ninth or tenth part of the produce which is currently derived from the land, yet since the proprietors of money lend considerable sums upon which they receive interest, whether by way of mortgages on land or the produce and commodities of the state, the sums owing to them usually exceed all the real money in the state, and they often become so powerful a body that they would in certain cases vie with the proprietors of land, if the latter were not often equally proprietors of money, and if the proprietors of large sums of money did not always seek to become also proprietors of land.

Nevertheless it is always true that all the sums which they have gained or saved have been derived from the land of the existing proprietors; but since numbers of these are ruined every day in a state, and since the others who acquire the ownership of their land take their place, the independence which the ownership of land affords applies only to those who retain the possession of it; and since all land always has a current master or proprietor, I always assume that it is from the property [*fond*] of the latter that all the inhabitants of the state derive their subsistence and all their wealth. If these proprietors all confined themselves to living on their revenues this would be beyond doubt, and in that case it would be much more difficult for the other inhabitants to enrich themselves at their expense.

Thus I will lay it down as a principle that the proprietors of land alone are naturally independent in a state: that all the other orders are dependent, whether as entrepreneurs or as people on wages, and that all the exchange and circulation of the state is conducted through the intermediacy of these entrepreneurs.

Francis Hutcheson

FOUR EXTRACTS FROM
A SYSTEM OF MORAL PHILOSOPHY
(1755)

Source: The four extracts are taken from the first edition of 1755, the detailed page references being respectively Vol. I, pp. 287–90; Vol. II, pp. 53–64; Vol. II, pp. 71–4; and Vol. II, pp. 318–21. Hutcheson's section numbers and paragraph summaries have been omitted, and the headings are the present editor's. Hutcheson's footnotes are keyed in by asterisks, and the present editor's by numerical indicators.

Francis Hutcheson (1694–1746), who held the Chair of Moral Philosophy at Glasgow University from 1730 until his death, appears to have exercised a significant influence on a number of the major figures of the Scottish Enlightenment— not least Adam Smith, who attended Hutcheson's lectures when he was a student at Glasgow (1737–40). The particular work of Hutcheson's from which our extracts are taken—*A System of Moral Philosophy*—was published posthumously in 1755, but it seems to have consisted quite largely of material which Hutcheson had used very much earlier in his lectures at Glasgow, so that Smith was probably familiar with its leading doctrines from his student days.

Passages dealing directly with economic matters are rather few and far between in Hutcheson's *System*, and the four extracts reproduced here contain the only really significant ones—apart, perhaps, from one or two on taxation. The first, on the division of labour (below, pp. 28–30), may possibly have had some influence on Smith, although there were numerous other contributions to this subject, both contemporary and ancient, upon which he could have drawn. It is noteworthy that the purposes for which Hutcheson used the idea—to demonstrate 'the necessity of living in society' and 'the great convenience of larger associations of men' (p. 30)—were very different from Smith's, and that Hutcheson's account makes no specific reference to the division of labour *in manufacture*.

The second extract, a more extensive piece on value and money (below, pp. 30–7), is fairly typical of its time and does not contain a great deal that is really original. Some of the individual statements which Hutcheson makes in the course of his treatment, however, may well have impressed Smith. For example, near the beginning of the section Hutcheson says:

> The natural ground of all value or price is some sort of use which goods afford in life; this is prerequisite to all estimation. But the prices or values in commerce do not

25

at all follow the real use or importance of goods for the support, or natural pleasure of life (p. 30).

Possibly this statement influenced the peculiar concept of 'value in use' implied in Smith's comment, in his famous water and diamonds example, that a diamond has 'scarce any value in use',[1] and, more generally, his view that 'value in use' (even in its more normal sense) could be regarded only as a pre-requisite of value in exchange and not as its determinant. Then again, there seems to be a distinct echo of Hutcheson's state-ment that 'a days digging or ploughing was as uneasy to a man a thousand years ago as it is now' (p. 33) in Smith's remark that 'equal quantities of labour, at all times and places, may be said to be of equal value to the labourer'—a remark which is vital to the understanding of his idea that labour alone, 'never varying in its own value', is the 'real price' of commodities.[2]

The most interesting part of this extract, perhaps, is the last two paragraphs, in which Hutcheson describes the various items which have to be added up in order to 'fix the price' of a commodity (below, pp. 36–7). These include not only 'the interest of money employed in trade', but also an allowance for the expense of the 'station of life' prescribed by the custom of the country for certain economic agents. 'This additional price of their labours', writes Hutcheson, 'is the just foundation of the ordinary profit of merchants, on which account they justly demand an higher price in selling, than what answers all that was expended upon the goods' (p. 37). Hutcheson realizes here that the price at which a commodity sells must provide a net income for the 'merchant', over and above 'the interest of money employed in trade', which is normally higher than the net remuneration received by wage-earners and indepen-dent artisans: the problem of the origin of profit is at least posed. But in his solution of this problem Hutcheson in-cludes all profit-receivers in the single category of 'merchants', and regards the 'ordinary profit' of this class as an 'additional price of their labours' rather than as an income associated with their use of capital in the employment of wage-labour. Clearly we are still in a Cantillonian—indeed, to some extent in a pre-

[1] *Wealth of Nations* (ed. E. Cannan, 6th edn., 1950), Vol. I, p. 33.
[2] ibid., Vol. I, p. 37.

Cantillonian—world, and the contrast which Smith was later to observe between the real world of his day and the fast-disappearing worlds of Cantillon and Hutcheson was no doubt at least partly responsible for the emergence of his own 'paradigm'.

The third extract, on interest (below, pp. 37–9), contains an important statement of the so-called 'fructification theory', which was quite often used in the eighteenth century to counteract the still-influential Aristotelian idea that since money was sterile (or, as Hutcheson put it (p. 38), 'not naturally fruitful'), interest was therefore not morally justifiable.[1] In 'trade', Hutcheson argues, 'men can make far greater gains by help of a large stock of money, than they could have made without it', and it is therefore 'but just' that the supplier of this money should receive a share of these gains 'equal at least to the profit he could have made by purchasing things naturally fruitful or yielding a rent' (p. 38). Hutcheson, to his credit, used this argument merely as a justification of the existence of interest and not as an explanation of its level, the latter being determined in his account by 'the state of trade, and the quantity of coin' (p. 38). The influence of the second of these two factors, which had been emphasized by several seventeenth-century writers, was denied or played down by Cantillon and many subsequent interest theorists (including Hume and Smith); and, of course, the normative elements which are evident in Hutcheson's treatment were bound to appear increasingly anachronistic as the century progressed. But his perceptive account of the interrelationships between the level of rent and that of interest is very reminiscent of the account which was later to be given by Turgot in his *Réflexions sur la Formation et la Distribution des Richesses;* and his statement that 'when many hands and much wealth are employed in trade . . . the profit made upon any given sum employed is smaller, and the interest the trader can afford must be less' (p. 138) anticipated the explanation of the secular fall in the rate of interest given by Joseph Massie,[2] and may possibly have

[1] cf. J. A. Schumpeter, *History of Economic Analysis* (1954), p. 332, footnote.
[2] cf. G. S. L. Tucker, *Progress and Profits in British Economic Thought, 1650–1850* (1960), p. 42.

influenced, either directly or indirectly, a somewhat similar passage in the *Wealth of Nations*.[1]

The fourth and final extract (below, pp. 40–1) contains a statement about the virtues of 'industry' and an attack on 'luxury'—themes which were fairly typical of their time, and which were increasingly stressed as the century progressed. The 'Mercantilist' integument in which these ideas appear in Hutcheson's formulation, however, had of course to be removed before they could be developed for use in the Smithian system.

A SYSTEM OF MORAL PHILOSOPHY

THE DIVISION OF LABOUR[2]

In the first place, 'tis obvious that for the support of human life, to allay the painful cravings of the appetites, and to afford any of those agreeable external enjoyments which our nature is capable of, a great many external things are requisite; such as food, cloathing, habitations, many utensils, and various furniture, which cannot be obtained without a great deal of art and labour, and the friendly aids of our fellows.

Again, 'tis plain that a man in absolute solitude, tho' he were of mature strength, and fully instructed in all our arts of life, could scarcely procure to himself the bare necessaries of life, even in the best soils or climates; much less could he procure any grateful conveniencies. One uninstructed in the arts of life, tho' he had full strength, would be still more incapable of subsisting in solitude: and it would be absolutely impossible, without a miracle, that one could subsist in this condition from his infancy. And suppose that food, raiment, shelter, and the means of sensual pleasure, were supplied by a miracle; yet a life in solitude must be full of fears and dangers. Suppose farther all these dangers removed; yet in solitude there could be no exercise

[1] *Wealth of Nations*, Vol. I, p. 375.
[2] This passage is extracted from Book II, Chapter iv, Hutcheson's title for the chapter being: '*The different* STATES *of* MEN. *The State of* LIBERTY *not a State of* WAR. *The Way that private* RIGHTS *are known. The Necessity of a* SOCIAL LIFE.'

for many of the natural powers and instincts of our species; no love, or social joys, or communication of pleasure, or esteem, or mirth. The contrary dispositions of soul must grow upon a man in this unnatural state, a sullen melancholy, and discontent, which must make life intolerable. This subject is abundantly explained by almost all authors upon the law of nature.

The mutual aids of a few in a small family, may procure most of the necessaries of life, and diminish dangers, and afford room for some social joys as well as finer pleasures. The same advantages could still be obtained more effectually and copiously by the mutual assistance of a few such families living in one neighbourhood, as they could execute more operose designs for the common good of all; and would furnish more joyful exercises of our social dispositions.

Nay 'tis well known that the produce of the labours of any given number, twenty, for instance, in providing the necessaries or conveniences of life, shall be much greater by assigning to one, a certain sort of work of one kind, in which he will soon acquire skill and dexterity, and to another assigning work of a different kind, than if each one of the twenty were obliged to employ himself, by turns, in all the different sorts of labour requisite for his subsistence, without sufficient dexterity in any. In the former method each procures a great quantity of goods of one kind, and can exchange a part of it for such goods obtained by the labours of others as he shall stand in need of. One grows expert in tillage, another in pasture and breeding cattle, a third in masonry, a fourth in the chace, a fifth in iron-works, a sixth in the arts of the loom, and so on throughout the rest. Thus all are supplied by means of barter with the works of complete artists. In the other method scarce any one could be dextrous and skilful in any one sort of labour.

Again some works of the highest use to multitudes can be effectually executed by the joint labours of many, which the separate labours of the same number could never have executed. The joint force of many can repel dangers arising from savage beasts or bands of robbers, which might have been fatal to many individuals were they separately to encounter them. The joint labours of twenty men will cultivate forests, or drain marshes, for farms to each one, and provide houses for habitation, and inclosures for their flocks, much sooner than the separate labours of the same number. By concert, and alternate relief, they can keep a perpetual watch, which without concert they could not accomplish.

Larger associations may further enlarge our means of enjoyment, and give more extensive and delightful exercise to our powers of every kind. The inventions, experience, and arts of multitudes are communicated; knowledge is increased, and social affections more diffused. Larger societies have force to execute greater designs of more lasting and extensive advantage.* These considerations abundantly shew the necessity of living in society, and obtaining the aid of our fellows, for our very subsistence; and the great convenience of larger associations of men for the improvement of life, and the increase of all our enjoyments.

VALUE AND MONEY[1]

In commerce it must often happen that one may need such goods of mine as yield a great and lasting use in life, and have cost a long course of labour to acquire and cultivate, while yet he has none of those goods I want in exchange, or not sufficient quantities; or what goods of his I want, may be such as yield but a small use, and are procurable by little labour. In such cases it cannot be expected that I should exchange with him. I must search for others who have the goods I want, and such quantities of them as are equivalent in use to my goods, and require as much labour to procure them; and the goods on both sides must be brought to some estimation or value.

The natural ground of all value or price is some sort of use which goods afford in life; this is prerequisite to all estimation. But the prices or values in commerce do not at all follow the real use or importance of goods for the support, or natural pleasure of life. By the wisdom and goodness of Providence there is such plenty of the means of support, and of natural pleasures, that their prices are much lower than of many other

* See this whole subject beautifully explained in the second book of *Cicero de Officiis*.

[1] This extract consists of the whole of Book II, Chapter xii, Hutcheson's title for the chapter being: '*The Values of* GOODS *in Commerce and the Nature of* COIN.'

things which to a wise man seem of little use. But when some aptitude to human use is presupposed, we shall find that the prices of goods depend on these two jointly, the *demand* on account of some use or other which many desire, and the *difficulty* of acquiring, or cultivating for human use. When goods are equal in these respects men are willing to interchange them with each other; nor can any artifice or policy make the values of goods depend on any thing else. When there is no *demand*, there is no price, were the *difficulty* of acquiring never so great: and were there no *difficulty* or labour requisite to acquire, the most universal *demand* will not cause a price; as we see in fresh water in these climates. Where the demand for two sorts of goods is equal, the prices are as the difficulty. Where the difficulty is equal, the prices are as the demand.

By the use causing a demand we mean not only a natural subserviency to our support, or to some natural pleasure, but any tendency to give any satisfaction, by prevailing custom or fancy, as a matter of ornament or distinction in the more eminent stations; for this will cause a demand as well as natural use. In like manner by difficulty of acquiring, we do not only mean great labour or toil, but all other circumstances which prevent a great plenty of the goods or performances demanded. Thus the price is encreased by the rarity or scarcity of the materials in nature, or such accidents as prevent plentiful crops of certain fruits of the earth; and the great ingenuity and nice taste requisite in the artists to finish well some works of art, as men of such genius are rare. The value is also raised, by the dignity of station in which, according to the custom of a country, the men must live who provide us with certain goods, or works of art. Fewer can be supported in such stations than in the meaner; and the dignity and expence of their stations must be supported by the higher prices of their goods or services. Some other* singular considerations may exceedingly heighten the values of goods to some men, which will not affect their estimation with others. These above mentioned are the chief which obtain in commerce.

In settling the values of goods for commerce, they must be reduced to some common measure on both sides. Such as

---

* *Pretium affectionis.* [Esteem value—Ed.]

'equal to the value of so many days labour, or to such quantities of grain, or to so many cattle of such a species, to such a measure or weight of certain fruits of the earth, to such weights of certain metals'. The standard or common measure would readily be taken in something of very common use for which there would be a general demand: and in fixing upon it different nations would according to their prudence or circumstances choose different materials.

The qualities requisite to the most perfect standard are these; it must be something generally desired so that men are generally willing to take it in exchange. The very making any goods the standard will of itself give them this quality. It must be portable; which will often be the case if it is rare, so that small quantities are of great value. It must be divisible without loss into small parts, so as to be suited to the values of all sorts of goods; and it must be durable, not easily wearing by use, or perishing in its nature. One or other of these prerequisites in the standard, shews the inconvenience of many of our commonest goods for that purpose. The man who wants a small quantity of my corn will not give me a work-beast for it, and his beast does not admit division. I want perhaps a pair of shoes, but my ox is of far greater value, and the other may not need him. I must travel to distant lands, my grain cannot be carried along for my support, without unsufferable expence, and my wine would perish in the carriage. 'Tis plain therefore that when men found any use for the rarer metals, silver and gold, in ornaments or utensils, and thus a demand was raised for them, they would soon also see that they were the fittest standards for commerce, on all the accounts above-mentioned. They are rare, and therefore a small quantity of them easily portable is equivalent to large quantities of other goods; they admit any divisions without loss; they are neither perishable, nor easily worn away by use. They are accordingly made standards in all civilized nations.

Metals have first been used as standards by quantity or weight, without coinage. This we see in antient histories, and in the* phrases of old languages. But this way was attended with two inconveniencies; one the trouble of making exact divisions,

* *Impendere, expendere nummos*, &c. [To weigh out, or lay out money —Ed.]

the other the uncertainty as to the purity of the metal. To prevent both, coinage has been introduced; in which pieces are made of very different well known sizes in the most convenient divisions: the quantity of pure metal in every piece is known; the finer methods of stamping secure us that they cannot be clipt or filed away without its being discernible at once. The publick faith of the state is interposed by these stamps, both for the quantity and purity, so that there is no occasion for assays or weighing, or making divisions.

These are the sole purposes of coinage. No stamp can add any considerable value, as it is easy workmanship in such valuable materials. But it may be good evidence for the value, when it is impressed by any just and wise authority. Trading nations cannot make the comparative value of their coin with respect to other goods, greater or less than the value of the metal, and of the easy workmanship of coinage. Coin is ever valued as a commodity in commerce, as well as other goods; and that in proportion to the rarity of the metal, for the demand is universal. A law can only fix or alter the legal denominations of pieces or ounces; and thus indeed affect, within the state, the legal claims formerly constituted in those denominations: but commerce will always follow the natural value. If one state had all the mines in the world in its power, then by circulating small quantities, it could make the values of these metals and coins high in respect of other goods; and by circulating more of them, it could make their values fall. We say indeed commonly, that the rates of labour and goods have risen since these metals grew plenty; and that the rates of labour and goods were low when the metals were scarce; conceiving the value of the metals as invariable, because the legal names of the pieces, the pounds, shillings, or pence, continue to them always the same till a law alters them. But a days digging or ploughing was as uneasy to a man a thousand years ago as it is now, tho' he could not then get so much silver for it: and a barrel of wheat, or beef, was then of the same use to support the human body, as it is now when it is exchanged for four times as much silver. Properly, the value of labour, grain, and cattle, are always pretty much the same, as they afford the same uses in life, where no new inventions of tillage, or pasturage, cause a greater quantity in proportion to the demand. 'Tis the metal chiefly that has undergone the great change of value, since these metals have been in greater plenty, the value of the coin is altered tho' it keeps the old names.

The governors of a state which has no monopoly of silver and gold, may change the names of their coins, and cheat their subjects, or put them into a state of cheating each other in their legal demands: but in commerce coin will retain the natural value of the metal in it, with little variation. Where the legal denominations of value are considerably changed, the effects are obvious at once; and in smaller changes the effects are proportionable, tho' not so sensible.

If the legal names of our crown pieces were doubled so that the ounce of silver were called ten shillings, the nominal prices of all goods would rise as much. We should not get the barrel of wheat for the new ten shillings, as we do now in cheap years: we must give the two ounces of silver as we do now, tho' they would be called twenty shillings. Suppose people so stupid that they were contented with the same names, but half the silver. Coining with any stamp is an easy manufacture, any nation could make our crown-pieces, and get for them double the quantity of our goods they got formerly. Our own merchant therefore gets for an ounce of silver from the farmer or manufacturer what formerly cost two ounces, and yet at foreign mercats he will get as many ounces for these goods as before. Now he doubles his first cost, beside his former profit. This vast gain would invite so many, and make such a demand, that the prices of all our goods would gradually rise, till they came to the same quantities of gold and silver they were at before, but with double nominal values; and then the new exorbitant gain would stop. At first our country would lose one half upon all goods bought from us by foreigners: this loss would fall upon men of estates and manufacturers at last.

As to foreign goods 'tis obvious the nominal prices of them must rise at once upon changing the names of our coin. Foreigners who do not regard our laws, or legal names of coin, must have for their goods the same pieces or ounces they got formerly. Our merchants therefore in selling these goods must have as many pieces or ounces, which now bear a double name.

Again, upon lowering the legal names of coin, the nominal prices of all goods must fall. The merchant cannot afford more pieces or ounces of metal, than he gave before for any goods to our farmer or manufacturer, as he will get no more at any foreign market, and this number now bears a smaller name. Foreign goods are bought abroad for the same ounces they were, and therefore the merchant can afford them here for the same ounces he formerly sold them at, and with the same profit, tho' the name be less. If one merchant refuses to sell so, another will, as all can afford it: or if all refuse, foreigners will send their goods into our country to be sold for the same ounces, now bearing a lower name.

'Tis a fundamental maxim about coin, that 'its value in commerce cannot be varied by names', that prices of goods keep their proportion to the quantities of metal, and not to the legal names. No man values a piece more than 'tis called twenty livres, or twenty Scots pounds, than he would have done on account of the Sterling name.

The changing considerably the legal names of coin must cause innumerable wrongs among the subjects of any state, since the real values of goods continue the same. The lowering of coins wrongs all who are indebted in legal denominations; they must pay more ounces of gold and silver than they received, or engaged for; and yet get no more ounces by any sales of their goods than they got formerly. All duties, taxes, rents, salaries payable in legal denominations are increased. More ounces are received by the creditors in such claims, and yet each ounce will purchase as much goods for the support or pleasure of life as before the change. The debtors therefore are so much wronged, and so much the creditors are unjustly enriched.

Raising the legal names has the like unjust effects on the other side. Debts, taxes, rents, salaries, specified in legal names, can then be discharged with fewer pieces or ounces; and yet the debtor gets as many ounces for any goods he sells as before; and the creditor can get no more of the goods necessary for life for an ounce than he got before. He is therefore so much wronged by the change made in the legal names.

The putting disproportioned values upon the several species of current coin must have bad effects on a country. The species under-valued at home will be carried abroad, and the species over-valued will be imported; as the former answers better at foreign markets, where the ounces of metal are regarded, and not the names, and the later answers best at home. Whatever sums are thus exchanged by foreigners, all their gain is so much loss to our country. What we export ourselves, hurts our country only by introducing perhaps a less convenient species. This disproportion often arises after the values were wisely fixed at the time they were made, if either the mines of one metal are more copious in proportion than those of the other; or there be a greater drain of one sort of metal by exportation, or by some consumption of it in the splendour of life.

An increase of both metals by copious mines, naturally abates the value of both, without any change of the names. And thus, properly speaking, the values of gold and silver are fallen within these two centuries above one half: tho' we more commonly say that the rates of goods are increased. Were the mines quite drained and the quantities of these metals much diminished by the various uses of them in plate, dress, and furniture, their value would rise again; or, we would vulgarly say, the rates of goods would fall. The standard itself is varying insensibly: and therefore if we would settle fixed salaries, which in all events would answer the same purposes of life, or support those entituled to them in the same condition with respect to others, they should neither be fixed in the legal names of coin, nor in a certain number of ounces of gold or silver. A decree of state may change the legal names; and the value of the ounces may alter by the increase or decrease of the quantities of these metals. Nor should such salaries be fixed in any quantities of more ingenious manufactures, for nice contrivances to facilitate labour, may lower the value of such goods. The most invariable salary would be so many days labour of men, or a fixed quantity of goods produced by the plain inartificial labours, such goods as answer the ordinary purposes of life. Quantities of grain come nearest to such a standard.

In matters of commerce to fix the price we should not only compute the first cost, freights, duties, and all expences made, along with the interest of money employed in trade, but the labours too, the care, attention, accounts, and correspondence about them; and in some cases take in also the condition of the person so employed, according to the custom of our country. The expence of his station of life must be defrayed by the price of such labours; and they deserve compensation as much as any other. This additional price of their labours is the just foundation of the ordinary profit of merchants, on which account they justly demand an higher price in selling, than what answers all that was expended upon the goods. Their value *here* is augmented by those labours, as justly as by those of farmers or artisans.

As there are many contingent losses by the perishing of some goods, or their receiving damage, these losses may be justly compensated by a further augmentation of the price of such as are safe. As merchants lose sometimes by the falling of the rates of goods on hand, they may justly take the contingent advantage too of goods on hand, when the rates of such goods rise by any accident which makes them scarce. Men who are fortunate in these accidents may be much enriched, without any fraud, or extortion. The constant profit is the just reward of their labours. Thus tho' the values of what is given and received in buying and selling should still be kept equal on both sides, as we shall see presently,[1] yet there is a natural gain in trade, viz. that additional price which the labour and attendance of the trader adds to the goods; and a contingent one, by the rising of prices.

INTEREST[2]

In loan for consumption at a set price or interest, the lender claims not the same individual, but equal quantities, and the price for the loan. Some goods bear natural fruits or increase, as lands, flocks, herds, gardens. The grant of these fruits naturally deserves a price or rent. Tho' goods have no fruits or increase, yet if they yield great convenience in life, and have cost such labour or expence as would have acquired goods naturally fruitful, if the proprietor grants the use of them, he may justly demand a price, such as he would have had if he had employed his money or labour on goods naturally fruitful. This is the case in setting of houses.

[1] Hutcheson makes this point in a section of the following chapter which is not included in these extracts.

[2] This passage is extracted from Book II, Chapter xiii, Hutcheson's title for the chapter being: ' *The Principal* CONTRACTS *in a* SOCIAL LIFE'.

If in any way of trade men can make far greater gains by help of a large stock of money, than they could have made without it, 'tis but just that he who supplies them with the money, the necessary means of this gain, should have for the use of it some share of the profit, equal at least to the profit he could have made by purchasing things naturally fruitful or yielding a rent. This shews the just foundation of interest upon money lent, tho' it be not naturally fruitful. Houses yield no fruits or increase, nor will some arable grounds yield any without great labour. Labour employed in managing money in trade, or manufactures, will make it as fruitful as any thing. Were interest prohibited, none would lend, except in charity; and many industrious hands, who are not objects of charity, would be excluded from large gains in a way very disadvantageous[1] to the publick.

The reasonable interest varies according to the state of trade, and the quantity of coin. In a country newly settled, or but beginning to trade, where few hands and little money are employed that way, great profits are made by small sums: and as in such places more land-rents are purchased for any given sum than in countries flourishing in trade, and abounding with money; an higher interest is reasonable, and no man would lend except upon an high interest. The gain too made by any sum is so large, that traders or purchasers can afford to give it. When many hands and much wealth are employed in trade, as men can be supported by smaller gains in proportion upon their large stocks, the profit made upon any given sum employed is smaller, and the interest the trader can afford must be less. As money grows plentier, and bears less interest in loans, more incline to purchases of lands than formerly; and this demand raises the rates of lands, so that smaller land-rents can be obtained for any sum. Men are therefore contented with smaller interest than formerly when they could have got greater land-rents. They should be satisfied if it surpasses the annual profits of purchases, as much as compensates the greater troubles or hazards attending the loans: and thus it falls of course, without the force of laws.

Laws too must follow these natural causes in settling the

[1] The original has 'advantageous', which would appear to be an error.

interest, otherways they will seldom have their effect, and be iniquitous. If the legal interest is high in wealthy nations, where small gains are made upon any given sum employed in trade, traders will not borrow without abatement of interest, nor will men borrow for purchasing lands, when the annual rents of them are far below the interest. Moneyed men may first run upon purchases, and decline to lend upon smaller than the legal interest; but the demand for lands will soon raise their price, so that they shall get much smaller annual rents for a given sum: many will therefore accept of interest below the legal, but higher than the annual rents of lands. If the legal interest is made too low, few will incline to lend; they will first attempt to purchase lands: if the price of them rise by the great demand, so that small annual profit is made this way, moneyed men will turn to trade and manufactures. Men not educated to such business, or who choose to live without business, will find active traders always fond of borrowing at higher than the legal interest, and will find ways by discount, and annual gifts agreed upon, to elude the law.

The chief use of such laws is to settle the interest decreed by courts on many occasions, where there has been no agreement of the parties; and to prevent the extortions of some grasping wretches upon the incautious, or the distressed. Prudent men will settle this point for themselves according to the natural causes.

If the polity of any state allows little commerce with foreigners, admits of no great increase of wealth in the hands of a few, nor of any alienation of lands to perpetuity; if it is design'd for a *republick of farmers*, which some great authors judge most adapted for virtue and happiness,* there all interest of money might properly be prohibited. But where the strength of a state depends on trade, such a law would be ruinous.

---

* This Harrington and others judge to be the polity of the Hebrews: and hence interest was prohibited among them, but it might be exacted from foreigners. Deut. xxiii. 19. Psalm xv. 5.

INDUSTRY, INTERNATIONAL TRADE, AND LUXURY[1]

Industry is the natural mine of wealth, the fund of all stores for exportation, by the surplus of which beyond the value of what a nation imports, it must increase in wealth and power. Diligent agriculture must furnish the necessaries of life, and the materials for all manufactures: and all mechanick arts should be encouraged to prepare them for use and exportation. Goods prepared for export should generally be free from all burdens and taxes, and so should the goods be which are necessarily consumed by the artificers, as much as possible; that no other country be able to undersell like goods at a foreign market. Where one country alone has certain materials, they may safely impose duties upon them when exported; but such moderate ones as shall not prevent the consumption of them abroad.

If a people have not acquired an habit of industry, the cheapness of all the necessaries of life rather incourages sloth. The best remedy is to raise the demand for all necessaries; not merely by premiums upon exporting them, which is often useful too; but by increasing the number of people who consume them: and when they are dear, more labour and application will be requisite in all trades and arts to procure them. Industrious foreigners should therefore be invited to us, and all men of industry should live with us unmolested and easy. Encouragement should be given to marriage, and to those who rear a numerous offspring to industry. The unmarried should pay higher taxes as they are not at the charge of rearing new subjects to the state. Any foolish notions of meanness in mechanick arts, as if they were unworthy of men of better families, should be borne down, and men of better condition as to birth or fortune engaged to be concerned in such occupations. Sloth should be punished by temporary servitude at least. Foreign materials should be imported and even premiums given, when necessary, that all our own hands may be employed; and that, by exporting them again manufactured, we may obtain from abroad the price of our labours. Foreign manufactures and

[1] This passage is extracted from Book III, Chapter ix, Hutcheson's title for the chapter being: '*Of the* NATURE *of* CIVIL LAWS *and their* EXECUTION.'

products ready for consumption, should be made dear to the consumer by high duties, if we cannot altogether prohibit the consumption; that they may never be used by the lower and more numerous orders of the people, whose consumption would be far greater than those of the few who are wealthy. Navigation, or the carriage of goods foreign or domestick, should be encouraged, as a gainful branch of business, surpassing often all the profit made by the merchant. This too is a nursery of fit hands for defence at sea.

'Tis vain to alledge that luxury and intemperance are necessary to the wealth of a state as they encourage all labour and manufactures by making a great consumption. It is plain there is no necessary vice in the consuming of the finest products, or the wearing of the dearest manufactures by persons whose fortunes can allow it consistently with all the duties of life. And what if men grew generally more frugal and abstemious in such things? more of these finer goods could be sent abroad: or if they could not, industry and wealth might be equally promoted by the greater consumption of goods less chargeable: as he who saves by abating of his own expensive splendour could by generous offices to his friends, and by some wise methods of charity to the poor, enable others to live so much better, and make greater consumption than was made formerly by the luxury of one. Five families supported in sober plenty may make vastly greater consumption for every good purpose, than one living in luxury. Younger children settled well with proper shares of a patrimony in sober plentiful families, may consume more than if an heir lived in all luxury, and the rest in indigence. And as to sobriety, it is generally true that it makes the greatest consumption. It makes men healthy and long livers. It enables men to marry soon and support numerous families. And consider even one alone: a sober plentiful consumption for sixty or seventy years is greater than a riotous one of ten or twelve, and of fifty more in beggary. Unless therefore a nation can be found where all men are already provided with all the necessaries and conveniencies of life abundantly, men may, without any luxury, make the very greatest consumption, by plentiful provision for their children, by generosity and liberality to kinsmen and indigent men of worth, and by compassion to the distresses of the poor.

David Hume

THREE EXTRACTS FROM
POLITICAL DISCOURSES
(1752)

Source: The first extract reprinted here—from Hume's essay *Of Commerce*—constitutes only about one-quarter of the original essay. The essays *Of Interest* and *Of the Balance of Trade*, on the other hand, are reprinted almost in their entirety, the passages omitted—which are noted at the appropriate points in the text—being relatively short. The texts used are based on those of the 1777 edition of Hume's *Essays and Treatises on Several Subjects* (which although posthumous is generally regarded as the definitive edition), as reproduced in *Essays Moral, Political, and Literary by David Hume* (ed. T. H. Green and T. H. Grose, 1889), Vol. I, pp. 293–5, 320–8, and 330–45. The Green and Grose texts have been checked independently against those of the 1777 edition, and a few minor corrections made. Hume's footnotes (as in the 1777 edition) are keyed in by symbols, and the present editor's by numerical indicators.

David Hume (1711–76), philosopher, historian, and economist, was one of the most influential polymaths of the eighteenth century. Most of his economic writings were contained in his *Political Discourses*, which was published in the same year (1752) as that in which Smith became Professor of Moral Philosophy at Glasgow University. Smith apparently read a paper on some of Hume's 'essays on commerce' to the Glasgow Literary Society very soon after their publication,[1] and there is no doubt that he appreciated their quality.

The essay *Of Commerce*, from which the first of our extracts (below, pp. 50–3) is taken, is interesting, first, because of Hume's historical-cum-sociological approach, which reminds one very much of Cantillon's. In an earlier part of the essay, not included in the extract, Hume sets the stage as follows:

> The bulk of every state may be divided into *husbandmen* and *manufacturers*. The former are employed in the culture of the land; the latter work up the materials furnished by the former, into all the commodities which are necessary or ornamental to human life. As soon as men quit their savage state, where they live chiefly by hunting and fishing, they must fall into these two classes; though the arts of agriculture employ *at first* the most numerous part of the society. Time and experience improve so much these arts, that the land may easily maintain a much greater number of men, than those who are immediately employed in its culture, or who furnish the more necessary manufactures to such as are so employed.[2]

The stadial view of the development of society which is adumbrated in this passage and elsewhere in the essay, and the

---

[1] See Jacob Viner, *Guide to John Rae's 'Life of Adam Smith'* (1965), pp. 53–8.
[2] *Essays Moral, Political, and Literary by David Hume* (ed. T. H. Green and T. H. Grose, 1889), Vol. I, p. 289. A footnote of Hume's has been omitted.

associated idea that 'manufacturers' are maintained 'by that superfluity, which arises from the labour of the farmers' (p. 51), were destined to become in one form or another the common property of almost all the great economists of the latter half of the century, whatever the particular 'paradigm' they professed.

The second interesting feature of the essay is the way in which the economic (and military) potentialities of the nation as a whole are visualized by Hume in terms of the disposition of its labour force. 'Every thing in the world', we read, 'is purchased by labour' (below, p. 50).[1] The 'labour of the farmers' produces a surplus which maintains those who labour in producing manufactured commodities, and many of the latter can if and when necessary be converted into soldiers. Thus 'the more labour . . . is employed beyond mere necessaries, the more powerful is any state; since the persons engaged in that labour may easily be converted to the public service' (p. 51), from which it follows that 'trade and industry are really nothing but a stock of labour' (p. 52).

The third feature is the attitude towards 'foreign commerce' expressed in the last paragraph of the extract, in which Hume argues that it ought to be looked upon with favour because it 'encreases the stock of labour in the nation' (below, p. 52). The interesting point here is that this effect will according to Hume be produced by a large export *and import* trade—an important modification of 'Mercantilist' theory, at any rate in some of its earlier formulations.

The essay *Of Interest* which follows in our extracts (below, pp. 53–61) represents perhaps Hume's most impressive performance in the economic field—not because any of the individual elements in his theory of interest are particularly original, but rather because of the ingenious blend of history, sociology, and economics in the analytical framework within which these elements are synthesized. The essay begins with a recapitulation of the quantity theory of money of which Hume had made use in the previous essay *Of Money* (not included in these extracts), and a categoric statement that 'the rate of interest . . . is not derived from the quantity of the precious metals'

[1] cf. *Wealth of Nations* (ed. E. Cannan, 6th edn., 1950), Vol. I, p. 35.

(p. 54). High interest, Hume proceeds to argue (p. 54), 'arises from *three* circumstances: A great demand for borrowing; little riches to supply that demand; and great profits arising from commerce ... Low interest, on the other hand, proceeds from the three opposite circumstances.'

Each of these three determinants, Hume goes on to claim, depends in its turn upon the 'habits and manners' which prevail among certain economic agents, and which themselves change as society develops and 'industry and commerce' increase. When a people emerges from the savage state, 'there must immediately arise an inequality of property', so that 'the *landed* interest is immediately established'. The 'habits and manners' of this landed class are such that 'the prodigals among them will always be more numerous than the misers', so that the 'demand for borrowing' will be great and the rate of interest high (below, p. 55).

The second determinant, too—'the great or little riches to supply the demand'—depends upon 'the habits and way of living of the people'. When society consists only of landlords and peasants, the stock of money in the country, however great or small it may be, is never 'collected in particular hands, so as to form considerable sums, or compose a great monied interest' (below, pp. 55–6). Thus the 'riches to supply the demand' are low, and interest remains high. Soon, however, 'another rank of men' arises—the artisans, who work up the materials supplied by the agricultural classes; and this increase in 'men's industry' eventually leads to the rise of yet another class—the 'merchants', among whom 'there is the same overplus of misers above prodigals, as, among the possessors of land, there is the contrary' (pp. 56–8). Through its 'frugality', this merchant class acquires great power over industry and amasses considerable sums of money, so that the increase in commerce 'by a necessary consequence, raises a great number of lenders, and by that means produces lowness of interest' (p. 59). And as a further consequence, it 'diminishes the profits arising from that profession', thereby giving rise to 'the *third* circumstance requisite to produce lowness of interest'. The main idea here is that when commerce has become 'extensive' the increased intensity of competition between merchants lowers the 'profits of trade', so that when they leave off business and seek 'an

47

annual and secure revenue' the merchants will 'accept more willingly of a low interest'. Low interest and low profits, Hume argues, 'both arise from an extensive commerce, and mutually forward each other. No man will accept of low profits, where he can have high interest; and no man will accept of low interest, where he can have high profits' (p. 59).

Smith accepted and incorporated into the *Wealth of Nations* a number of the elements of this account, notably Hume's attack on the 'monetary' theories of the decline of the interest rate (to which Smith specifically referred his readers),[1] and his view that increased intensity of competition lowers the rate of profit on capital.[2] But in the *Wealth of Nations* the question of what determined the rate of profit became one of great importance in its own right, rather than a mere appendage to the problem of what determined the rate of interest[3]—and it was not merely the profits of the 'merchants' (at any rate in the narrower sense of that word) which were a matter of concern. From the point of view of the shaping of the *Wealth of Nations*, indeed, it is arguable that the main influence of Hume's essay *Of Interest* lay not in any of its specific arguments but in the 'sociological' methodology lying behind its general approach.[4]

The essay *Of the Balance of Trade* (below, pp. 61–73), with which our extracts conclude, contains Hume's famous theory of the specie-flow adjustment mechanism in international trade. This essay is addressed to those who have 'a strong jealousy with regard to the balance of trade, and a fear, that all their gold and silver may be leaving them' (p. 62). Hume's argument, in effect, is that a nation never need be apprehensive of losing its money if it preserves its people and its industry, because there exists an automatic economic mechanism which 'must for ever, in all neighbouring countries, preserve money nearly proportionable to the art and industry of each nation'

[1] *Wealth of Nations*, Vol. I, p. 376.

[2] ibid., pp. 98 and 375. Smith's view of the mechanism through which a declining rate of profit led to a declining rate of interest, however, had rather more in common with the accounts given by Cantillon, Hutcheson, and Massie than with that given by Hume.

[3] cf. G. S. L. Tucker, *Progress and Profits in British Economic Thought, 1650–1850* (1960), p. 63, where this point is very well stated.

[4] It is possible, however, that Smith's theory of saving and investment may have owed something to *Of Interest*.

(p. 64). If a country loses money the prices of its goods will fall, its exports will rise, and the money it has lost will flow back to it again. If a country gains money the prices of its goods will rise, its exports will fall, its imports of foreign commodities (which are now comparatively cheap) will rise, and the money it has gained will flow out from it again (pp. 63–4). Through this simple mechanism, money, like water, finds its own level. Since it can never fall below this level, it is absurd to interfere with the freedom of trade for fear of losing your specie; and since it can never rise above this level, it is equally absurd to interfere with it in the hope of accumulating specie (p. 71).

It is often said that Adam Smith made no reference at all in the *Wealth of Nations* to this self-regulating mechanism in terms of changing price levels, and this alleged circumstance is proclaimed as 'one of the mysteries of the history of economic thought'.[1] In actual fact, however, Smith *did* make fairly explicit reference to it in his discussion of bounties, using Hume's own illustration of Spain and Portugal (below, pp. 64–5) and Hume's own analogy of the water heaped up 'beyond its proper level' (p. 65), and emphasizing the fact that any 'degradation in the value of silver' caused by 'the political institutions of a particular country' would enable foreign nations 'to undersell them, not only in the foreign, but even in the home market'.[2] The only 'mystery' is why Smith did not afford the theory a more prominent place—and this really is not much of a mystery at all. Smith, while commending the ingenuity of the theory to his Glasgow students, felt that Hume's exposition tended a little towards 'the notion that public opulence consists in money'[3]—which it undoubtedly did, particularly in the section of the essay dealing with paper money (pp. 68–70). He also no doubt felt that Hume overemphasized the role of movements in prices as the key factor in the process of adjustment; that there were various other

---

[1] Jacob Viner, *Studies in the Theory of International Trade* (1937), p. 87; cf. J. A. Schumpeter, *History of Economic Analysis* (1954), p. 367, and W. L. Taylor, *Francis Hutcheson and David Hume as Predecessors of Adam Smith* (1965), pp. 131–3.

[2] *Wealth of Nations*, Vol. II pp. 16–19; cf. Smith's *Lectures on Justice Police, Revenue and Army* (ed. E. Cannan, 1896), pp. 201–3.

[3] Smith, *Lectures on Justice, etc.*, p. 197.

factors involved, especially if one was looking at the problem in the context of the long-run development of the economy; and that Hume's theory, at any rate as he had formulated it in the essay, took too little account of the lags and frictions which attended the working of the mechanism in the real world.

POLITICAL DISCOURSES

OF COMMERCE

Where manufactures and mechanic arts are not cultivated, the bulk of the people must apply themselves to agriculture; and if their skill and industry encrease, there must arise a great superfluity from their labour beyond what suffices to maintain them. They have no temptation, therefore, to encrease their skill and industry; since they cannot exchange that superfluity for any commodities, which may serve either to their pleasure or vanity. A habit of indolence naturally prevails. The greater part of the land lies uncultivated. What is cultivated, yields not its utmost for want of skill and assiduity in the farmers. If at any time the public exigencies require, that great numbers should be employed in the public service, the labour of the people furnishes now no superfluities, by which these numbers can be maintained. The labourers cannot encrease their skill and industry on a sudden. Lands uncultivated cannot be brought into tillage for some years. The armies, mean while, must either make sudden and violent conquests, or disband for want of subsistence. A regular attack or defence, therefore, is not to be expected from such a people, and their soldiers must be as ignorant and unskilful as their farmers and manufacturers.

Every thing in the world is purchased by labour; and our passions are the only causes of labour. When a nation abounds in manufactures and mechanic arts, the proprietors of land, as well as the farmers, study agriculture as a science, and redouble their industry and attention. The superfluity, which arises from their labour, is not lost; but is exchanged with manufactures for those commodities, which men's luxury now makes them covet. By this means, land furnishes a great deal more of the necessaries of life, than what suffices for those who cultivate it. In times of peace and tranquillity, this superfluity goes to the maintenance of manufacturers, and the improvers of liberal arts. But it is easy for the public to convert many of these manufacturers into soldiers, and maintain them by that superfluity, which arises from the labour of the farmers. Accordingly we find, that this is the case in all civilized governments. When the sovereign raises an army, what is the consequence? He imposes a tax. This tax obliges all the people to retrench what is least necessary to their subsistence. Those, who labour in such commodities, must either enlist in the troops, or turn themselves to agriculture, and thereby oblige some labourers to enlist for want of business. And to consider the matter abstractedly, manufacturers encrease the power of the state only as they store up so much labour, and that of a kind to which the public may lay claim, without depriving any one of the necessaries of life. The more labour, therefore, is employed beyond mere necessaries, the more powerful is any state; since the persons engaged in that labour may easily be converted to the public service. In a state without manufacturers, there may be the same number of hands; but there is not the same quantity of labour, nor of the same kind. All the labour is there bestowed upon necessaries, which can admit of little or no abatement.

Thus the greatness of the sovereign and the happiness of the state are, in a great measure, united with regard to trade and manufactures. It is a violent method, and in most cases impracticable, to oblige the labourer to toil, in order to raise from the land more than what subsists himself and family. Furnish him with manufactures and commodities, and he will do it of himself. Afterwards you will find it easy to seize some part of his superfluous labour, and employ it in the public service, without giving him his wonted return. Being accustomed to industry, he will think this less grievous, than if, at once, you obliged him to an augmentation of labour without any reward. The case is the same with regard to the other members of the state. The greater is the stock of labour of all kinds, the greater quantity may be taken from the heap, without making any sensible alteration in it.

A public granary of corn, a storehouse of cloth, a magazine

of arms; all these must be allowed real riches and strength in any state. Trade and industry are really nothing but a stock of labour, which, in times of peace and tranquillity, is employed for the ease and satisfaction of individuals; but in the exigencies of state, may, in part, be turned to public advantage. Could we convert a city into a kind of fortified camp, and infuse into each breast so martial a genius, and such a passion for public good, as to make every one willing to undergo the greatest hardships for the sake of the public; these affections might now, as in ancient times, prove alone a sufficient spur to industry, and support the community. It would then be advantageous, as in camps, to banish all arts and luxury; and, by restrictions on equipage and tables, make the provisions and forage last longer than if the army were loaded with a number of super-fluous retainers. But as these principles are too disinterested and too difficult to support, it is requisite to govern men by other passions, and animate them with a spirit of avarice and industry, art and luxury. The camp is, in this case, loaded with a superfluous retinue; but the provisions flow in proportionably larger. The harmony of the whole is still supported; and the natural bent of the mind being more complied with, individuals, as well as the public, find their account in the observance of those maxims.

The same method of reasoning will let us see the advantage of *foreign* commerce, in augmenting the power of the state, as well as the riches and happiness of the subject. It encreases the stock of labour in the nation; and the sovereign may convert what share of it he finds necessary to the service of the public. Foreign trade, by its imports, furnishes materials for new manufactures; and by its exports, it produces labour in particular commodities, which could not be consumed at home. In short, a kingdom, that has a large import and export, must abound more with industry, and that employed upon delicacies and luxuries, than a kingdom which rests contented with its native commodities. It is, therefore, more powerful, as well as richer and happier. The individuals reap the benefit of these commodities, so far as they gratify the senses and appetites. And the public is also a gainer, while a greater stock of labour is, by this means, stored up against any public exigency; that is, a greater number of laborious men are maintained, who may be diverted to the public service, without robbing any one of the necessaries, or even the chief conveniencies of life.

OF INTEREST

Nothing is esteemed a more certain |sign of the flourishing condition of any nation than the lowness of interest: And with reason; though I believe the cause is somewhat different from what is commonly apprehended. Lowness of interest is generally ascribed to plenty of money. But money, however plentiful, has no other effect, *if fixed*, than to raise the price of labour. Silver is more common than gold; and therefore you receive a greater quantity of it for the same commodities. But do you pay less interest for it? Interest in BATAVIA and JAMAICA is at 10 *per cent.* in PORTUGAL at 6; though these places, as we may learn from the prices of every thing, abound more in gold and silver than either LONDON or AMSTERDAM

Were all the gold in ENGLAND annihilated at once, and one and twenty shillings substituted in the place of every guinea, would money be more plentiful or interest lower? No surely: We should only use silver instead of gold. Were gold rendered as common as silver, and silver as common as copper; would money be more plentiful or interest lower? We may assuredly give the same answer. Our shillings would then be yellow, and our halfpence white; and we should have no guineas. No other difference would ever be observed; no alteration on commerce, manufactures, navigation, or interest; unless we imagine, that the colour of the metal is of any consequence.

Now, what is so visible in these greater variations of scarcity or abundance in the precious metals, must hold in all inferior changes. If the multiplying of gold and silver fifteen times makes no difference, much less can the doubling or tripling them. All augmentation has no other effect than to heighten the price of labour and commodities; and even this variation is little more than that of a name. In the progress towards these changes, the augmentation may have some influence, by exciting industry; but after the prices are settled, suitably to the new abundance of gold and silver, it has no manner of influence.[1]

An effect always holds proportion with its cause. Prices have risen near four times since the discovery of the INDIES; and it is probable gold and silver have multiplied much more: But interest has not fallen much above half. The rate of interest, therefore, is not derived from the quantity of the precious metals.

Money having chiefly a fictitious value, the greater or less plenty of it is of no consequence, if we consider a nation within itself; and the quantity of specie, when once fixed, though ever so large, has no other effect, than to oblige every one to tell out a greater number of those shining bits of metal, for clothes, furniture or equipage, without encreasing any one convenience of life. If a man borrow money to build a house, he then carries home a greater load; because the stone, timber, lead, glass, &c. with the labour of the masons and carpenters, are represented by a greater quantity of gold and silver. But as these metals are considered chiefly as representations, there can no alteration arise, from their bulk or quantity, their weight or colour, either upon their real value or their interest. The same interest, in all cases, bears the same proportion to the sum. And if you lent me so much labour and so many commodities; by receiving five *per cent*. you always receive proportional labour and commodities, however represented, whether by yellow or white coin, whether by a pound or an ounce. It is in vain, therefore, to look for the cause of the fall or rise of interest in the greater or less quantity of gold and silver, which is fixed in any nation.

High interest arises from *three* circumstances: A great demand for borrowing; little riches to supply that demand; and great profits arising from commerce: And these circumstances are a clear proof of the small advance of commerce and industry, not of the scarcity of gold and silver. Low interest, on the other hand, proceeds from the three opposite circumstances: A small demand for borrowing; great riches to supply that demand; and small profits arising from commerce: And these

[1] The ideas in this paragraph are spelt out in more detail in Hume's essay *Of Money*, which immediately precedes *Of Interest* in the published collections, but which is not included in these extracts.

circumstances are all connected together, and proceed from the encrease of industry and commerce, not of gold and silver. We shall endeavour to prove these points; and shall begin with the causes and the effects of a great or small demand for borrowing.

When a people have emerged ever so little from a savage state, and their numbers have encreased beyond the original multitude, there must immediately arise an inequality of property; and while some possess large tracts of land, others are confined within narrow limits, and some are entirely without any landed property. Those who possess more land than they can labour, employ those who possess none, and agree to receive a determinate part of the product. Thus the *landed* interest is immediately established; nor is there any settled government, however rude, in which affairs are not on this footing. Of these proprietors of land, some must presently discover themselves to be of different tempers from others; and while one would willingly store up the produce of his land for futurity, another desires to consume at present what should suffice for many years. But as the spending of a settled revenue is a way of life entirely without occupation; men have so much need of somewhat to fix and engage them, that pleasures, such as they are, will be the pursuit of the greater part of the landholders, and the prodigals among them will always be more numerous than the misers. In a state, therefore, where there is nothing but a landed interest, as there is little frugality, the borrowers must be very numerous, and the rate of interest must hold proportion to it. The difference depends not on the quantity of money, but on the habits and manners which prevail. By this alone the demand for borrowing is encreased or diminished. Were money so plentiful as to make an egg be sold for sixpence; so long as there are only landed gentry and peasants in the state, the borrowers must be numerous, and interest high. The rent for the same farm would be heavier and more bulky: But the same idleness of the landlord, with the higher price of commodities, would dissipate it in the same time, and produce the same necessity and demand for borrowing.

Nor is the case different with regard to the *second* circumstance which we proposed to consider, namely, the great or little riches to supply the demand. This effect also depends on

the habits and way of living of the people, not on the quantity
of gold and silver. In order to have, in any state, a great number of lenders, it is not sufficient nor requisite, that there be
great abundance of the precious metals. It is only requisite,
that the property or command of that quantity, which is in the
state, whether great or small, should be collected in particular
hands, so as to form considerable sums, or compose a great
monied interest. This begets a number of lenders, and sinks
the rate of usury; and this I shall venture to affirm, depends
not on the quantity of specie, but on particular manners and
customs, which make the specie gather into separate sums or
masses of considerable value.

For suppose, that, by miracle, every man in GREAT BRITAIN
should have five pounds slipt into his pocket in one night;
this would much more than double the whole money that is at
present in the kingdom; yet there would not next day, nor for
some time, be any more lenders, nor any variation in the interest. And were there nothing but landlords and peasants in
the state, this money, however abundant, could never gather
into sums; and would only serve to encrease the prices of every
thing, without any farther consequence. The prodigal landlord
dissipates it, as fast as he receives it; and the beggarly peasant
has no means, nor view, nor ambition of obtaining above a bare
livelihood. The overplus of borrowers above that of lenders
continuing still the same, there will follow no reduction of
interest. That depends upon another principle; and must
proceed from an encrease of industry and frugality, of arts and
commerce.

Every thing useful to the life of man arises from the ground;
but few things arise in that condition which is requisite to
render them useful. There must, therefore, beside the peasants
and the proprietors of land, be another rank of men, who
receiving from the former the rude materials, work them into
their proper form, and retain part for their own use and subsistence. In the infancy of society, these contracts between the
artisans and the peasants, and between one species of artisans
and another are commonly entered into immediately by the
persons themselves, who, being neighbours, are easily acquainted with each other's necessities, and can lend their mutual assistance to supply them. But when men's industry

encreases, and their views enlarge, it is found, that the most remote parts of the state can assist each other as well as the more contiguous, and that this intercourse of good offices may be carried on to the greatest extent and intricacy. Hence the origin of *merchants*, one of the most useful races of men, who serve as agents between those parts of the state, that are wholly unacquainted, and are ignorant of each other's necessities. Here are in a city fifty workmen in silk and linen, and a thousand customers; and these two ranks of men, so necessary to each other, can never rightly meet, till one man erects a shop, to which all the workmen and all the customers repair. In this province, grass rises in abundance: The inhabitants abound in cheese, and butter, and cattle; but want bread and corn, which, in a neighbouring province, are in too great abundance for the use of the inhabitants. One man discovers this. He brings corn from the one province and returns with cattle; and supplying the wants of both, he is, so far, a common benefactor. As the people encrease in numbers and industry, the difficulty of their intercourse encreases: The business of the agency or merchandize becomes more intricate; and divides, subdivides, compounds, and mixes to a greater variety. In all these transactions, it is necessary, and reasonable, that a considerable part of the commodities and labour should belong to the merchant, to whom, in a great measure, they are owing. And these commodities he will sometimes preserve in kind, or more commonly convert into money, which is their common representation. If gold and silver have encreased in the state together with the industry, it will require a great quantity of these metals to represent a great quantity of commodities and labour. If industry alone has encreased, the prices of every thing must sink, and a small quantity of specie will serve as a representation.

There is no craving or demand of the human mind more constant and insatiable than that for exercise and employment; and this desire seems the foundation of most of our passions and pursuits. Deprive a man of all business and serious occupation, he runs restless from one amusement to another; and the weight and oppression, which he feels from idleness, is so great, that he forgets the ruin which must follow him from his immoderate expences. Give him a more harmless way of employing his mind or body, he is satisfied, and feels no longer that insatiable thirst after pleasure. But if the employment you give him be lucrative, especially if the profit be attached to every particular exertion of industry, he has gain so often in his eye, that he acquires, by degrees, a passion for it, and knows no such pleasure as that of seeing the daily encrease of his fortune. And this is the reason why trade encreases frugality, and why, among merchants, there is the same overplus of misers above prodigals, as, among the possessors of land, there is the contrary.

Commerce encreases industry, by conveying it readily from one member of the state to another, and allowing none of it to perish or become useless. It encreases frugality, by giving occupation to men, and employing them in the arts of gain, which soon engage their affection, and remove all relish for pleasure and expense. It is an infallible consequence of all industrious professions, to beget frugality, and make the love of gain prevail over the love of pleasure. Among lawyers and physicians who have any practice, there are many more who live within their income, than who exceed it, or even live up to it. But lawyers and physicians beget no industry; and it is even at the expence of others they acquire their riches; so that they are sure to diminish the possessions of some of their fellow-citizens, as fast as they encrease their own. Merchants, on the contrary, beget industry, by serving as canals to convey it through every corner of the state: And at the same time, by their frugality, they acquire great power over that industry, and collect a large property in the labour and commodities, which they are the chief instruments in producing. There is no other profession, therefore, except merchandize, which can make the monied interest considerable, or, in other words, can encrease industry, and, by also encreasing frugality, give a great command of that industry to particular members of the society. Without commerce, the state must consist chiefly of landed gentry, whose prodigality and expence make a continual demand for borrowing; and of peasants, who have no sums to supply that demand. The money never gathers into large stocks or sums, which can be lent at interest. It is dispersed into numberless hands, who either squander it in idle show and magnificence, or employ it in the purchase of the common necessaries of life. Commerce alone assembles it into considerable sums; and this effect it has merely from the industry which it begets, and the frugality which it inspires, independent of that particular quantity of precious metal which may circulate in the state.

Thus an encrease of commerce, by a necessary consequence, raises a great number of lenders, and by that means produces lowness of interest. We must now consider how far this encrease of commerce diminishes the profits arising from that profession, and gives rise to the *third* circumstance requisite to produce lowness of interest.

It may be proper to observe on this head, that low interest and low profits of merchandize are two events, that mutually forward each other, and are both originally derived from that extensive commerce, which produces opulent merchants, and renders the monied interest considerable. Where merchants possess great stocks, whether represented by few or many pieces of metal, it must frequently happen, that, when they either become tired of business, or leave heirs unwilling or unfit to engage in commerce, a great proportion of these riches naturally seeks an annual and secure revenue. The plenty diminishes the price, and makes the lenders accept of a low interest. This consideration obliges many to keep their stock employed in trade, and rather be content with low profits than dispose of their money at an under-value. On the other hand, when commerce has become extensive, and employs large stocks, there must arise rivalships among the merchants, which diminish the profits of trade, at the same time that they encrease the trade itself. The low profits of merchandize induce the merchants to accept more willingly of a low interest, when they leave off business, and begin to indulge themselves in ease and indolence. It is needless, therefore, to enquire which of these circumstances, to wit, *low interest or low profits*, is the cause, and which the effect? They both arise from an extensive commerce, and mutually forward each other. No man will accept of low profits, where he can have high interest; and no man will accept of low interest, where he can have high profits. An extensive commerce, by producing large stocks, diminishes both interest and profits; and is always assisted, in its diminution of the one, by the proportional sinking of the other. I may add, that, as low profits arise from the encrease of commerce and industry, they serve in their turn to its farther encrease, by rendering the commodities cheaper, encouraging the consumption, and heightening the industry. And thus, if we consider the whole connexion of causes and effects, interest is the barometer of the state, and its lowness is a sign almost infallible of the flourishing condition of a people. It proves the encrease of industry, and its prompt circulation through the whole state, little inferior to a demonstration. And though, perhaps, it may not be impossible but a sudden and a great check to commerce may have a momentary effect of the same kind, by throwing so many stocks out of trade; it must be attended with such misery and want of employment in the poor, that, besides its short duration, it will not be possible to mistake the one case for the other.

Those who have asserted, that the plenty of money was the cause of low interest, seem to have taken a collateral effect for a cause; since the same industry, which sinks the interest, commonly acquires great abundance of the precious metals. A variety of fine manufactures, with vigilant enterprising merchants, will soon draw money to a state, if it be any where to be found in the world. The same cause, by multiplying the conveniencies of life, and encreasing industry, collects great riches into the hands of persons, who are not proprietors of land, and produces, by that means, a lowness of interest. But though both these effects, plenty of money and low interest, naturally arise from commerce and industry, they are altogether independent of each other. For suppose a nation removed into the *Pacific* ocean, without any foreign commerce, or any knowledge of navigation: Suppose, that this nation possesses always the same stock of coin, but is continually encreasing in its numbers and industry: It is evident, that the price of every commodity must gradually diminish in that kingdom; since it is the proportion between money and any species of goods, which fixes their mutual value; and, upon the present supposition, the conveniencies of life become every day more abundant, without any alteration in the current specie. A less quantity of money, therefore, among this people, will make a rich man, during the times of industry, than would suffice to that purpose, in ignorant and slothful ages. Less money will build a house, portion a daughter, buy an estate, support a manufactory, or maintain a family and equipage. These are the uses for which men borrow money; and therefore, the greater or less quantity of it in a state has no influence on the interest. But it is evident, that the greater or less stock of labour and commodities must have a great influence; since we really and in effect borrow these, when we take money upon interest. It is true, when commerce is extended all over the globe, the most industrious nations always abound most with the precious metals: So that low interest and plenty of money are in fact almost inseparable. But still it is of consequence to know the principle whence any phenomenon arises, and to distinguish between a cause and a concomitant effect. Besides that the speculation is curious, it may frequently be of use in the conduct of public affairs. At least, it must be owned, that nothing can be of more use than to improve, by practice, the method of reasoning on these subjects, which of all others are the most important; though they are commonly treated in the loosest and most careless manner.

[' *Another reason of this popular mistake with regard to the cause of low interest*', *Hume proceeds*, ' *seems to be the instance of some nations; where, after a sudden acquisition of money or of the precious metals, by means of foreign conquest, the interest has fallen . . .*' *The five concluding paragraphs of the essay, in which Hume explores this theme, are here omitted.*]

OF THE BALANCE OF TRADE

It is very usual, in nations ignorant of the nature of commerce, to prohibit the exportation of commodities, and to preserve among themselves whatever they think valuable and useful. They do not consider, that, in this prohibition, they act directly contrary to their intention; and that the more is exported of any commodity, the more will be raised at home, of which they themselves will always have the first offer.

It is well known to the learned, that the ancient laws of ATHENS rendered the exportation of figs criminal; that being supposed a species of fruit so excellent in ATTICA, that the ATHENIANS deemed it too delicious for the palate of any foreigner. And in this ridiculous prohibition they were so much in earnest, that informers were thence called *sycophants* among them, from two GREEK words, which signify *figs* and *discoverer*.* There are proofs in many old acts of parliament of the same ignorance in the nature of commerce, particularly in the reign of EDWARD III. And to this day, in FRANCE, the exportation of corn is almost always prohibited; in order, as they say, to prevent famines; though it is evident, that nothing contributes more to the frequent famines, which so much distress that fertile country.

The same jealous fear, with regard to money, has also prevailed among several nations; and it required both reason and experience to convince any people, that these prohibitions serve to no other purpose than to raise the exchange against them, and produce a still greater exportation.

These errors, one may say, are gross and palpable: But there still prevails, even in nations well acquainted with commerce, a strong jealousy with regard to the balance of trade, and a fear, that all their gold and silver may be leaving them. This seems to me, almost in every case, a groundless apprehension; and I should as soon dread, that all our springs and rivers should be exhausted, as that money should abandon a kingdom where there are people and industry. Let us carefully preserve these latter advantages; and we need never be apprehensive of losing the former.

It is easy to observe, that all calculations concerning the balance of trade are founded on very uncertain facts and suppositions. The custom-house books are allowed to be an insufficient ground of reasoning; nor is the rate of exchange much better; unless we consider it with all nations, and know also the proportions of the several sums remitted; which one may safely pronounce impossible. Every man, who has ever reasoned on this subject, has always proved his theory, whatever it was, by facts and calculations, and by an enumeration of all the commodities sent to all foreign kingdoms.

The writings of Mr. Gee[1] struck the nation with an universal

* PLUT. *De Curiositate.*

[1] Joshua Gee was a contributor to the *British Merchant*, and the author of (inter alia) *The Trade and Navigation of Great Britain Considered* (1729).

panic, when they saw it plainly demonstrated, by a detail of particulars, that the balance was against them for so considerable a sum as must leave them without a single shilling in five or six years. But luckily, twenty years have since elapsed, with an expensive foreign war; yet is it commonly supposed, that money is still more plentiful among us than in any former period.

Nothing can be more entertaining on this head than Dr SWIFT; an author so quick in discerning the mistakes and absurdities of others. He says, in his *short view of the state of* IRELAND,[1] that the whole cash of that kingdom formerly amounted but to 500,000*l.*; that out of this the IRISH remitted every year a neat million to ENGLAND, and had scarcely any other source from which they could compensate themselves, and little other foreign trade than the importation of FRENCH wines, for which they paid ready money. The consequence of this situation, which must be owned to be disadvantageous, was, that, in a course of three years, the current money of IRELAND, from 500,000*l.* was reduced to less than two. And at present, I suppose, in a course of 30 years it is absolutely nothing. Yet I know not how, that opinion of the advance of riches in IRELAND, which gave the Doctor so much indignation, seems still to continue, and gain ground with every body.

In short, this apprehension of the wrong balance of trade, appears of such a nature, that it discovers itself, wherever one is out of humour with the ministry, or is in low spirits; and as it can never be refuted by a particular detail of all the exports, which counterbalance the imports, it may here be proper to form a general argument, that may prove the impossibility of this event, as long as we preserve our people and our industry.

Suppose four-fifths of all the money in GREAT BRITAIN to be annihilated in one night, and the nation reduced to the same condition, with regard to specie, as in the reigns of the HARRYS and EDWARDS, what would be the consequence? Must not the price of all labour and commodities sink in proportion, and every thing be sold as cheap as they were in those ages? What nation could then dispute with us in any foreign market, or

---

[1] Published in 1728.

pretend to navigate or to sell manufactures at the same price, which to us would afford sufficient profit? In how little time, therefore, must this bring back the money which we had lost, and raise us to the level of all the neighbouring nations? Where, after we have arrived, we immediately lose the advantage of the cheapness of labour and commodities; and the farther flowing in of money is stopped by our fulness and repletion.

Again, suppose, that all the money of GREAT BRITAIN were multiplied fivefold in a night, must not the contrary effect follow? Must not all labour and commodities rise to such an exorbitant height, that no neighbouring nations could afford to buy from us; while their commodities, on the other hand, became comparatively so cheap, that, in spite of all the laws which could be formed, they would be run in upon us, and our money flow out; till we fall to a level with foreigners, and lose that great superiority of riches, which had laid us under such disadvantages?

Now, it is evident, that the same causes, which would correct these exorbitant inequalities, were they to happen miraculously, must prevent their happening in the common course of nature, and must for ever, in all neighbouring nations, preserve money nearly proportionable to the art and industry of each nation. All water, wherever it communicates, remains always at a level. Ask naturalists the reason; they tell you, that, were it to be raised in any one place, the superior gravity of that part not being balanced, must depress it, till it meet a counterpoise; and that the same cause, which redresses the inequality when it happens, must for ever prevent it, without some violent external operation.*

Can one imagine, that it had ever been possible, by any laws, or even by any art or industry, to have kept all the money in SPAIN, which the galleons have brought from the INDIES? Or that all commodities could be sold in FRANCE for a tenth of the price which they would yield on the other side of the

---

* There is another cause, though more limited in its operation, which checks the wrong balance of trade, to every particular nation to which the kingdom trades. When we import more goods than we export, the exchange turns against us, and this becomes a new encouragement to export; as much as the charge of carriage and insurance of the money which becomes due would amount to. For the exchange can never rise but a little higher than that sum.

PYRENEES, without finding their way thither, and draining from that immense treasure? What other reason, indeed, is there, why all nations, at present, gain in their trade with SPAIN and PORTUGAL; but because it is impossible to heap up money, more than any fluid, beyond its proper level? The sovereigns of these countries have shown, that they wanted not inclination to keep their gold and silver to themselves, had it been in any degree practicable.

But as any body of water may be raised above the level of the surrounding element, if the former has no communication with the latter; so in money, if the communication be cut off, by any material or physical impediment, (for all laws alone are ineffectual) there may, in such a case, be a very great inequality of money. Thus the immense distance of CHINA, together with the monopolies of our INDIA companies, obstructing the communication, preserve in EUROPE the gold and silver, especially the latter, in much greater plenty than they are found in that kingdom. But, notwithstanding this great obstruction, the force of the causes abovementioned is still evident. The skill and ingenuity of EUROPE in general surpasses perhaps that of CHINA, with regard to manual arts and manufactures; yet are we never able to trade thither without great disadvantage. And were it not for the continual recruits, which we receive from AMERICA, money would soon sink in EUROPE, and rise in CHINA, till it came nearly to a level in both places. Nor can any reasonable man doubt, but that industrious nation, were they as near us as POLAND or BARBARY, would drain us of the overplus of our specie, and draw to themselves a larger share of the WEST INDIAN treasures. We need not have recourse to a physical attraction, in order to explain the necessity of this operation. There is a moral attraction, arising from the interests and passions of men, which is full as potent and infallible.

How is the balance kept in the provinces of every kingdom among themselves, but by the force of this principle, which makes it impossible for money to lose its level, and either to rise or sink beyond the proportion of the labour and commodities which are in each province? Did not long experience make people easy on this head, what a fund of gloomy reflections might calculations afford to a melancholy YORKSHIREMAN,

while he computed and magnified the sums drawn to LONDON
by taxes, absentees, commodities, and found on comparison
the opposite articles so much inferior? And no doubt, had the
Heptarchy subsisted in ENGLAND, the legislature of each state
had been continually alarmed by the fear of a wrong balance;
and as it is probable that the mutual hatred of these states
would have been extremely violent on account of their close
neighbourhood, they would have loaded and oppressed all
commerce, by a jealous and superfluous caution. Since the
union has removed the barriers between SCOTLAND and
ENGLAND, which of these nations gains from the other by this
free commerce? Or if the former kingdom has received any
encrease of riches, can it reasonably be accounted for by any
thing but the encrease of its art and industry? It was a common
apprehension in ENGLAND, before the union, as we learn from
L'ABBE DU BOS,* that SCOTLAND would soon drain them of
their treasure, were an open trade allowed; and on the other
side the TWEED a contrary apprehension prevailed: With what
justice in both, time has shown.

What happens in small portions of mankind, must take place
in greater. The provinces of the ROMAN empire, no doubt,
kept their balance with each other, and with ITALY, independent of the legislature; as much as the several countries of
GREAT BRITAIN, or the several parishes of each country.
And any man who travels over EUROPE at this day, may see,
by the prices of commodities, that money, in spite of the
absurd jealousy of princes and states, has brought itself nearly
to a level; and that the difference between one kingdom and
another is not greater in this respect, than it is often between
different provinces of the same kingdom. Men naturally flock
to capital cities, sea-ports, and navigable rivers. There we find
more men, more industry, more commodities, and consequently more money; but still the latter difference holds proportion with the former, and the level is preserved.†

* *Les interets d'*ANGLETERRE *malentendus.*
† It must carefully be remarked, that throughout this discourse,
wherever I speak of the level of money, I mean always its proportional
level to the commodities, labour, industry, and skill, which is in the
several states. And I assert, that where these advantages are double,
triple, quadruple, to what they are in the neighbouring states, the

Our jealousy and our hatred of FRANCE are without bounds; and the former sentiment, at least, must be acknowledged reasonable and well-grounded. These passions have occasioned innumerable barriers and obstructions upon commerce, where we are accused of being commonly the aggressors. But what have we gained by the bargain? We lost the FRENCH market for our woollen manufactures, and transferred the commerce of wine to SPAIN and PORTUGAL, where we buy worse liquor at a higher price. There are few ENGLISHMEN who would not think their country absolutely ruined, were FRENCH wines sold in ENGLAND so cheap and in such abundance as to supplant, in some measure, all ale, and home-brewed liquors: But would we lay aside prejudice, it would not be difficult to prove, that nothing could be more innocent, perhaps advantageous. Each new acre of vineyard planted in FRANCE, in order to supply ENGLAND with wine, would make it requisite for the FRENCH to take the produce of an ENGLISH acre, sown in wheat or barley, in order to subsist themselves; and it is evident, that we should thereby get command of the better commodity.

There are many edicts of the FRENCH king, prohibiting the planting of new vineyards, and ordering all those which are lately planted to be grubbed up: So sensible are they, in that country, of the superior value of corn, above every other product.

Mareschal VAUBAN complains often, and with reason, of the absurd duties which load the entry of those wines of LANGUE-DOC, GUIENNE, and other southern provinces, that are imported into BRITANNY and NORMANDY. He entertained no doubt but these latter provinces could preserve their balance, notwithstanding the open commerce which he recommends. And it is evident, that a few leagues more navigation to ENGLAND would

---

money infallibly will also be double, triple, quadruple. The only circumstances that can obstruct the exactness of these proportions, is the expense of transporting the commodities from one place to another; and this expense is sometimes unequal. Thus the corn, cattle, cheese, butter, of DERBYSHIRE, cannot draw the money of LONDON, so much as the manufactures of LONDON draw the money of DERBYSHIRE. But this objection is only a seeming one: For so far as the transport of commodities is expensive, so far is the communication between the places obstructed and imperfect.

make no difference; or if it did, that it must operate alike on the commodities of both kingdoms.

There is indeed one expedient by which it is possible to sink, and another by which we may raise money beyond its natural level in any kingdom; but these cases, when examined, will be found to resolve into our general theory, and to bring additional authority to it.

I scarcely know any method of sinking money below its level, but those institutions of banks, funds, and paper-credit, which are so much practised in this kingdom. These render paper equivalent to money, circulate it throughout the whole state, make it supply the place of gold and silver, raise proportionably the price of labour and commodities, and by that means either banish a great part of those precious metals, or prevent their farther encrease. What can be more short-sighted than our reasonings on this head? We fancy, because an individual would be much richer, were his stock of money doubled, that the same good effect would follow were the money of every one encreased; not considering, that this would raise as much the price of every commodity, and reduce every man, in time, to the same condition as before. It is only in our public negociations and transactions with foreigners, that a greater stock of money is advantageous; and as our paper is there absolutely insignificant, we feel, by its means, all the ill effects arising from a great abundance of money, without reaping any of the advantages.*

Suppose that there are 12 millions of paper, which circulate in the kingdom as money, (for we are not to imagine, that all our enormous funds are employed in that shape) and suppose the real cash of the kingdom to be 18 millions: Here is a state which is found by experience to be able to hold a stock of 30 millions. I say, if it be able to hold it, it must of necessity have acquired it in gold and silver, had we not obstructed the

---

* We observed in Essay III.[1] that money, when encreasing, gives encouragement to industry, during the interval between the encrease of money and rise of the prices. A good effect of this nature may follow too from paper-credit; but it is dangerous to precipitate matters, at the risk of losing all by the failing of that credit, as must happen upon any violent shock in public affairs.

[1] The essay *Of Money*.

entrance of these metals by this new invention of paper. *Whence would it have acquired that sum?* From all the kingdoms of the world. *But why?* Because, if you remove these 12 millions, money in this state is below its level, compared with our neighbours; and we must immediately draw from all of them, till we be full and saturate, so to speak, and can hold no more. By our present politics, we are as careful to stuff the nation with this fine commodity of bank-bills and chequer-notes, as if we were afraid of being overburthened with the precious metals.

It is not to be doubted, but the great plenty of bullion in FRANCE is, in a great measure, owing to the want of paper-credit. The FRENCH have no banks: Merchants bills do not there circulate as with us: Usury or lending on interest is not directly permitted; so that many have large sums in their coffers: Great quantities of plate are used in private houses; and all the churches are full of it. By this means, provisions and labour still remain cheaper among them, than in nations that are not half so rich in gold and silver. The advantages of this situation, in point of trade as well as in great public emergencies, are too evident to be disputed.

The same fashion a few years ago prevailed in GENOA, which still has place in ENGLAND and HOLLAND, of using services of CHINA-ware instead of plate; but the senate, foreseeing the consequence, prohibited the use of that brittle commodity beyond a certain extent; while the use of silver-plate was left unlimited. And I suppose, in their late distresses, they felt the good effect of this ordinance. Our tax on plate is, perhaps, in this view, somewhat impolitic.

Before the introduction of paper-money into our colonies, they had gold and silver sufficient for their circulation. Since the introduction of that commodity, the least inconveniency that has followed is the total banishment of the precious metals. And after the abolition of paper, can it be doubted but money will return, while these colonies possess manufactures and commodities, the only thing valuable in commerce, and for whose sake alone all men desire money.

What pity LYCURGUS did not think of paper-credit, when he wanted to banish gold and silver from SPARTA! It would have served his purpose better than the lumps of iron he made use of as money; and would also have prevented more effectually all commerce with strangers, as being of so much less real and intrinsic value.

[Two long paragraphs, first introduced in the 1764 edition of the Essays and Treatises, *are omitted here. They deal with the advantages, as well as the disadvantages, accruing from certain recent practices of Scottish banks in relation to the granting of credit.]*

But as our projects of paper-credit are almost the only expedient, by which we can sink money below its level; so, in my opinion, the only expedient, by which we can raise money above it, is a practice which we should all exclaim against as destructive, namely, the gathering of large sums into a public treasure, locking them up, and absolutely preventing their circulation. The fluid, not communicating with the neighbouring element, may, by such an artifice, be raised to what height we please. To prove this, we need only return to our first supposition, of annihilating the half or any part of our cash; where we found, that the immediate consequence of such an event would be the attraction of an equal sum from all the neighbouring kingdoms. Nor does there seem to be any necessary bounds set, by the nature of things, to this practice of hoarding. A small city, like GENEVA, continuing this policy for ages, might engross nine-tenths of the money of EUROPE. There seems, indeed, in the nature of man, an invincible obstacle to that immense growth of riches. A weak state, with an enormous treasure, will soon become a prey to some of its poorer, but more powerful neighbours. A great state would dissipate its wealth in dangerous and ill-concerted projects; and probably destroy, with it, what is much more valuable, the industry, morals, and numbers of its people. The fluid, in this case, raised to too great a height, bursts and destroys the vessel that contains it; and mixing itself with the surrounding element, soon falls to its proper level.

So little are we commonly acquainted with this principle, that, though all historians agree in relating uniformly so recent an event, as the immense treasure amassed by HARRY VII. (which they make amount to 2,700,000 pounds,) we rather reject their concurring testimony, than admit of a fact, which agrees so ill with our inveterate prejudices. It is indeed probable, that this sum might be three-fourths of all the money in ENGLAND. But where is the difficulty in conceiving, that such a sum might be amassed in twenty years, by a cunning, rapacious, frugal, and almost absolute monarch? Nor is it probable, that the diminution of circulating money was ever sensibly felt by the people, or ever did them any prejudice. The sinking of the prices of all commodities would immediately replace it, by giving ENGLAND the advantage in its commerce with the neighbouring kingdoms.

[Five paragraphs containing historical illustrations are omitted here.]

From these principles we may learn what judgment we ought to form of those numberless bars, obstructions, and imposts, which all nations of Europe, and none more than ENGLAND, have put upon trade; from an exorbitant desire of amassing money, which never will heap up beyond its level, while it circulates; or from an ill-grounded apprehension of losing their specie, which never will sink below it. Could any thing scatter our riches, it would be such impolitic contrivances. But this general ill effect, however, results from them, that they deprive neighbouring nations of that free communication and exchange which the Author of the world has intended, by giving them soils, climates, and geniuses, so different from each other.

Our modern politics embrace the only method of banishing money, the using of paper-credit; they reject the only method of amassing it, the practice of hoarding; and they adopt a hundred contrivances, which serve to no purpose but to check industry, and rob ourselves and our neighbours of the common benefits of art and nature.

All taxes, however, upon foreign commodities, are not to be regarded as prejudicial or useless, but those only which are founded on the jealousy above-mentioned. A tax on German linen encourages home manufactures, and thereby multiplies our people and industry. A tax on brandy encreases the sale of rum, and supports our southern colonies. And as it is necessary, that imposts should be levied, for the support of government, it may be thought more convenient to lay them on foreign commodities, which can easily be intercepted at the port, and subjected to the impost. We ought, however, always to remember the maxim of Dr. SWIFT, that, in the arithmetic of the customs, two and two make not four, but often make only one.[1] It can scarcely be doubted, but if the duties on wine were lowered to a third, they would yield much more to the government than at present: Our people might thereby afford to drink commonly a better and more wholesome liquor; and no prejudice would ensue to the balance of trade, of which we are so jealous. The manufacture of ale beyond the agriculture is but inconsiderable, and gives employment to few hands. The transport of wine and corn would not be much inferior.

But are there not frequent instances, you will say, of states and kingdoms, which were formerly rich and opulent, and are now poor and beggarly? Has not the money left them, with which they formerly abounded? I answer, If they lose their trade, industry, and people, they cannot expect to keep their gold and silver: For these precious metals will hold proportion to the former advantages. When LISBON and AMSTERDAM got the EAST-INDIA trade from VENICE and GENOA, they also got the profits and money which arose from it. Where the seat of government is transferred, where expensive armies are maintained at a distance, where great funds are possessed by foreigners; there naturally follows from these causes a diminution of the specie. But these, we may observe, are violent and forcible methods of carrying away money, and are in time commonly attended with the transport of people and industry. But where these remain, and the drain is not continued, the money always finds its way back again, by a hundred canals, of which we have no notion or suspicion. What immense treasures have been spent, by so many nations, in FLANDERS, since the revolution, in the course of three long wars? More money perhaps than the half of what is at present in EUROPE. But what has now become of it? Is it in the narrow compass of the AUSTRIAN provinces? No, surely: It has most of it returned to the several countries whence it came, and has followed

[1] The 'maxim' to which Hume refers here will be found in Swift's *An Answer to a Paper called a Memorial* (1728).

that art and industry, by which at first it was acquired. For above a thousand years, the money of EUROPE has been flowing to ROME, by an open and sensible current; but it has been emptied by many secret and insensible canals: And the want of industry and commerce renders at present the papal dominions the poorest territory in all ITALY.

In short, a government has great reason to preserve with care its people and its manufactures. Its money, it may safely trust to the course of human affairs, without fear or jealousy. Or if it ever give attention to this latter circumstance, it ought only to be so far as it affects the former.

A. R. J. Turgot

VALUE AND MONEY
(Circa 1769)

Source: This piece has been translated from the text of Turgot's manuscript draft, as reproduced in *Œuvres de Turgot* (ed. G. Schelle), Vol. III (1919), pp. 79–98. There are no omissions. All the footnotes are the present editor's.

A. R. J. Turgot (1727–81) spent most of his life in the service of the French Crown, eventually rising—although only for a very brief period—to the high office of *Contrôleur Général des Finances*. To historians of economic thought he is known mainly for his great work *Réflexions sur la Formation et la Distribution des Richesses*, written probably in 1766 and published in a Physiocratic journal three years later.

In the present collection, however, Turgot is represented not by the *Réflexions*, but by his lesser-known unfinished essay on *Value and Money*. The origins of this essay, which did not see the light of day until Du Pont unearthed the manuscript and published it in his edition of Turgot's collected works in 1808, are to some extent wrapped in mystery. Turgot mentions in the essay a work by Graslin published in 1767, which he says has 'just appeared' (below, p. 89); and in a letter to Du Pont dated 20 February 1770 he refers to something he has written on 'the principles of the determination of value'.[1] It seems a fair bet, then, that the essay was written at some time between 1767 and 1770—quite possibly, as Du Pont claimed, for a projected *Dictionnaire du Commerce*, the prospectus for which appeared in 1769 but which never in fact got off the ground.[2]

The germ of a number of the ideas in the essay is to be found in two sections of the *Réflexions* where Turgot deals with the way in which prices or values are placed on goods in the course of trade.[3] In the *Réflexions*, these sections are merely a prolegomenon to a discussion of money; in the essay, by way of contrast, the opening section on money is merely a prolegomenon to the discussion of value which constitutes the main—and by far the more profound—part of the work. Turgot may well have realized, after writing the *Réflexions*, and possibly after reading Graslin's book, that the subject of value was much more

[1] *Œuvres de Turgot* (ed. G. Schelle), Vol. III (1919), p. 379.
[2] cf. Schelle's footnote on p. 79 of Vol. III of his edition of Turgot's *Œuvres*.
[3] In my *Turgot on Progress, Sociology and Economics* (1973), the sections concerned are translated on pp. 135–6.

fundamental than he had thought, and therefore seized the next occasion which offered—the invitation from the editor of the *Dictionnaire du Commerce*—in order to develop his ideas on it.

The 'primary foundation' of the values which are fixed on commodities in the course of trade, Turgot argues, is 'that quality of goodness [*bonté*] in relation to our needs by which the gifts and goods of nature are regarded as adapted to our enjoyments, to the satisfaction of our desires' (below, p. 85)—i.e., their utility, or use value. He begins his analysis by showing how a man in isolation would gradually learn 'to compare his needs with one another, and to regulate his search for objects . . . in accordance with the order of the necessity and utility of his different needs' (p. 87); and then proceeds to argue that the degree of esteem which this man attaches to each object (its 'esteem value', as Turgot calls it) will be 'precisely that portion of the total of his resources which corresponds to the desire he has for this object, or that portion which he is willing to employ to satisfy this desire' (p. 89).[1] A second man is now brought into the picture, and in his analysis of the exchanges which will take place between the two men Turgot endeavours to show that an 'average esteem value' (which he calls 'appraisal value') is formed, and that this in its turn determines 'the *price* or the condition of the exchange' (pp. 90–3). In the final section of the article, he brings in two more men, and the essay breaks off in the middle of a discussion of the exchange transactions which will then take place between them.

Many authors before Turgot had explained value in terms of the interaction between 'utility' and 'scarcity', including in the latter concept not only the varying degree in which nature provides the commodities concerned but also the varying quantity of resources (or 'labour') required to produce them.[2]

---

[1] cf. Hannah R. Sewell, *The Theory of Value before Adam Smith* (1901), p. 101: 'The merit of Turgot's explanation is that it shows that cost affects value, by first limiting desire.'

[2] One of the most notable of these authors was Galiani, to whose *Della Moneta* (1751) Turgot specifically refers in his essay (below, p. 189). An English translation of certain key sections of *Della Moneta* will be found in *Early Economic Thought* (ed. A. E. Monroe, 1945), pp. 281–99. A more complete French translation, by G. H. Bousquet and J. Crisafulli, was published in 1955. The passage referred to by Turgot appears on pp. 85–6 of the latter work.

Turgot's essay, in effect, attempts to incorporate 'scarcity' into 'utility'—or, putting it another way, to 'reduce' the former to the latter—and by this means to base exchange value primarily on utility.[1] It can hardly be said that his effort was conspicuously successful: precisely at the most crucial points in his analysis the argument becomes tortuous and unclear, and it may well be that the essay remained unfinished not because the project for the *Dictionnaire du Commerce* was abandoned but because Turgot could not see any way round the difficulties involved. The alternative approach to the value problem—via the quantity of resources (or 'labour') required to produce the commodity—which Smith adopted, following a tradition which was at that time stronger in Britain than on the Continent, was destined to win out for almost a century. What is interesting is that Turgot's attempt was in fact made, and that a man of his calibre should have believed that a utility-based theory of value was perfectly compatible with a 'paradigm' not essentially dissimilar from Smith's.

VALUE AND MONEY

Money has this in common with all species of measures, that it is a kind of language which differs, among different peoples, in everything which is arbitrary and conventional, but of which the different forms are drawn together and rendered identical, in some respects, through their relation to a common term or standard.

This common term which draws all languages together, and which inevitably causes all tongues to be basically similar to one another in spite of the diversity of the sounds which they employ, is nothing other than the very ideas which the words express, that is, the objects of nature which are represented by the senses to the human mind and the notions which men have

[1] Hannah R. Sewell (op. cit., p. 106) claims that Turgot gave the 'labour element' a fundamental position, 'making it the ultimate measure and determiner not only of exchange value but also of personal or private value'. Surely, however, the amount of labour required to procure a commodity is with Turgot merely one of the factors which a man has to take into account, as a datum, in deciding what portion of his resources he is *willing* to employ in order to obtain it.

formed for themselves in distinguishing the different aspects of these objects and in combining them in a thousand ways.

It is this common basis, essential to all languages independently of all convention, which allows us to take each language, each system of conventions adopted as the signs of ideas, and to compare it with every other system of conventions, just as we would compare the system of ideas itself which may be interpreted in each tongue with that originally expressed in every other—which allows us, in a word, *to translate*.

The common term of all measures of length, area, and capacity is nothing other than extent itself, the different measures of which adopted by different peoples are only arbitrary divisions, which can in like manner be compared and reduced to one another.

We translate from one language into another; we reduce one measure to another. These different expressions indicate two very different operations.

Languages designate ideas by sounds which are in themselves foreign to these ideas. These sounds, as between one language and another, are entirely different, and in order to explain them we have to substitute one sound for another sound: for the sound of the foreign language, the corresponding sound of the language into which one is translating. Measures, on the other hand, measure extent only by means of extent itself. The only arbitrary and variable thing here is the choice of the quantity of extent which it has been decided to take as the unit, and the divisions which have been adopted to make the different measures understood. Thus there is no question of one thing having to be substituted for another; there are only quantities to be compared, and relations to be substituted for other relations.

The common term to which the *money* of all nations is related is the *value* of all the objects of trade which it serves to measure. But since this value cannot be designated except by the quantity of money to which it corresponds, it follows that we cannot *evaluate* [*évaluer*] one kind of *money* except in terms of another kind of *money*, just as we cannot interpret the sounds of a language except by other sounds.

Since the money of all civilized nations is made of the same materials, and since the different kinds of money differ from one another, like the measures, only by reason of the divisions of these materials and the arbitrary determination of what is regarded as the unit, they are capable, from this point of view, of being reduced to one another, just as the measures used by different nations are.

We shall see in what follows that this reduction is made in a very convenient way, through the expression of their weight and fineness.

But this way of evaluating money through the expression of its weight and fineness is not enough to make the language of trade understood so far as money is concerned. All the nations of Europe are familiar with two kinds of money. In addition to *real money* like the écu, the louis, the crown, and the guinea, which are pieces of metal, stamped with a well-known impression, and which are current under these denominations, each nation has created a kind of *fictitious money* [*monnaie fictive*], which is called *money of account*, or numerary money, whose denominations and divisions, although they do not correspond to any piece of real money, form a common scale to which real money is related by evaluating it in terms of the number of parts of this scale to which it corresponds. Such is in France the livre of account, or numerary livre, composed of twenty sous, of which each is subdivided into twelve deniers. There is no piece of money which corresponds to a livre; but an écu is worth three livres; a louis is worth twenty-four livres; and the expression of the value of these two kinds of real money in terms of a money of account establishes the relation of the écu to the louis as one to eight.

This money of account, since it consists, as we have seen, only of simple arbitrary denominations, varies from one nation to another, and within the same nation it may vary from one period to another.

The English also have their livre [pound] sterling, divided into twenty sous or shillings, which are divided into twelve deniers or pence. The Dutch reckon in florins, whose divisions do not correspond at all to those of our livre.

Thus in *commercial geography* we have to be made aware not only of the real money of each nation and its evaluation in weight and fineness, but also of the money of account employed by each nation, the relation of this money of account to the real money which is current in the nation, and the relation which the moneys of account of different nations have with one another.

The relation between the money of account and the real money of each nation is determined by expressing the value of the real money in terms of the money of account of the country concerned: of the ducat in terms of florins, of the guinea in terms of shillings and pence sterling, and of the louis and the écu in terms of *tournois* livres.[1]

So far as the relation which the moneys of account used by different nations have with one another is concerned, the idea which first presents itself is to deduce it from the relation of the money of account of each country to the real money, and from one's knowledge of the weight and fineness of the latter. Indeed, if we know the weight and fineness of an English crown and the weight and fineness of a French écu, we will know the relation of the crown to the French écu, and knowing how much the écu is worth in terms of *tournois* deniers, we can work out from this what the crown is worth in terms of *tournois* deniers. And since we also know what the crown is worth in terms of pence sterling, we know that such and such a number of pence sterling is equivalent to such and such a number of *tournois* deniers, and we then have the relation of the pound sterling to the *tournois* livre.

This way of evaluating the moneys of account of different nations by comparing them with the real money of each nation and using our knowledge of the weight and fineness of the latter, would not be subject to any difficulty if money were made of one metal alone—silver, for example—or if the relative value of the different metals employed for this purpose—of gold and silver, for example—were the same in all trading nations, that is, if some weight or other of fine gold, one mark for example, were worth exactly a particular number of grains of fine silver which was the same in all nations. But this relative value of gold and silver varies according to the relative abundance or scarcity of these two metals in the different nations.

If, in a nation, there is thirteen times as much silver as there is gold, and consequently thirteen marks of silver are given for one mark of gold, fourteen marks of silver will be given for one

---

[1] The *livre tournois* was the livre (of 20 sous) minted at Tours.

mark of gold in some other nation where there is fourteen times as much silver as there is gold. It follows from this that if, in order to determine the value of the moneys of account of two nations in which gold and silver do not have the same relative value—in order to evaluate, for example, the pound sterling in terms of *tournois* livres—we use gold money as the term of comparison, we will not get the same result as if we had used silver money. It is clear that the true evaluation will lie between these two results; but, in order to determine it rigorously and with complete precision, it would be necessary in solving the problem to take account of a whole number of very difficult considerations. Nevertheless, in monetary transactions between nations, all the negotiations relative to these transactions, the representation of money by bills of credit [*papiers de crédit*], and the operations of exchange and banking, presuppose that this problem has been solved.

The word *money*, in its proper, original, and simple sense, which corresponds exactly to the Latin *moneta*, means a piece of metal of a weight and fineness which are determined and guaranteed by the impression which the public authorities have caused to be put on it. To give the name, to describe the impression, and to state the weight and fineness of each kind of money of the different nations, reducing this weight to the number of marks—that is all that has to be done in order to give a clear idea of money considered under this first point of view.

But usage has conferred on this word *money* a broader and more abstract acceptation. The metals are divided into pieces of a certain weight; the authorities guarantee their fineness by means of an impression only in order to enable them to be used with convenience and safety in trade, in order that they should serve there at the same time as measures of value and as a representative pledge of commodities; moreover, men were minded to divide the metals in this way, to mark them, to make them, in a word, into *money*, only because these metals were already serving as measure and common pledge of all values.

Money having no other employment, this word has been regarded as designating that employment itself; and, as it is true to say that money is the measure and pledge of values, and as everything which is a measure and pledge of values can take the place of money, the word money has been applied in a broad sense to everything which is used for this purpose. It is in this sense that it is said that cowries are the money of the Maldive Islands; that cattle constituted the money of the Germans and the ancient inhabitants of Latium; that gold, silver, and copper are the money of civilized peoples; and that these metals constituted money before men had thought of designating their weight and fineness by means of a legal impression. It is in this sense that we give to the bills of credit which represent money the name of *paper money*. It is in this sense, finally, that the word money is applicable to the purely abstract denominations which serve for the mutual comparison of all values, even those of real money, and which are called *money of account, bank money*, etc.

The word *money*, in this sense, ought never to be translated by the Latin word *moneta*, but by the word *pecunia*, to which it corresponds very exactly.

It is in this latter sense, as measure of values and pledge of commodities, that we are going to envisage *money*, in tracing the course of its introduction into trade and the progress which the art of *measuring values* has made among men.

First of all, it is necessary to obtain a clear idea of what ought to be understood here by this word *value*.[1]

This abstract noun, which corresponds to the verb *valoir*, in Latin *valere*, has in common parlance several meanings between which it is important to distinguish.

In the original sense which this word had in the Latin language it meant strength or vigour; *valere* also meant *to be in good health*, and in French we still retain this early sense in the derivatives *valide, invalide*, and *convalescence*. Starting from this acceptation, in which the word *value* meant strength, its

[1] Here, and throughout the essay, the French noun *valeur* has been translated as 'value', the important point in the present context being that both words have the same dual meaning—value *in use* and value *in exchange*—in which Turgot is particularly interested. The French verb *valoir* (to be worth, to possess worth or value, to be equivalent to), however, has quite often been left as it is, in order not to obscure a linguistic point which Turgot is making. An English translation has been added in square brackets in some places in order to make the point clearer.

sense was twisted to make it mean military courage, a virtue which ancient peoples have almost always designated by the same word, which signified bodily strength.[1]

The word *valoir* has in the French language assumed another sense in which it is very often used, and which, although different from the acceptation which is given in trade to this word and to the word *value*, nevertheless constitutes its primary foundation.

It expresses that quality of goodness [*bonté*] in relation to our needs by which the gifts and goods of nature are regarded as adapted to our enjoyments, to the satisfaction of our desires. We say that a ragout *ne vaut rien* [is of no worth or value, is no good] when it tastes bad; that a certain food *ne vaut rien* [is of no worth or value, is bad] for the health; or that one material *vaut mieux* [is of more worth or value, is better] than another material—an expression which has no connection with *commercial value* and signifies only that it is more adapted to the uses for which it is intended.

The adjectives *bad, mediocre, good,* and *excellent* characterize the different degrees of this kind of *value*. Nevertheless, we should note that the noun *value* is not used anything like as often in this sense as the verb *valoir*. But when we do make use of it, we can mean by it only the quality of goodness of an object relatively to our enjoyments. Although this quality of goodness is always relative to ourselves, we nevertheless have in mind, in applying the word *value* to it, a real quality which is intrinsic in the object and by virtue of which it is suitable for our use.

This sense of the word *value* would be appropriate for a man in isolation, without any communication with other men.

Let us imagine this man exercising his faculties[2] only in respect of a single object; he will search for it, avoid it, or show no interest in it and leave it alone. In the first case, he has no doubt a motive for searching for this object: he judges it suitable for his enjoyment; he will find it *good*, and this relative

---

[1] cf. the English word 'valour'.

[2] *Facultés*. This word may mean 'faculties' in the sense of abilities, powers, or aptitudes, and it may also mean 'resources' in the sense of the means at one's disposal. A little further on, as will be seen, Turgot begins to use it in the latter sense.

quality of goodness might be given the absolute name of *value*. But this *value*, which is not being compared at all with other *values*, would not be capable of being measured at all, and the thing which *vaut* [possesses worth] would not be *evaluated* at all.

If the same man has a choice between several objects which are suitable for his use, he may prefer one to another; he may find an orange more pleasant than chestnuts, or a fur better for protecting him from the cold than a piece of cotton cloth. He will judge that one of these things *vaut mieux* [is of more worth or value, is better] than another; he will compare in his mind, he will appraise, *their values*. He will make up his mind, in consequence, to concern himself with the things he prefers and to leave the others alone.

A savage has killed a calf which he is taking to his hut: on the way he comes across a deer; he kills it and takes it in place of the calf, in the expectation of eating more delicate meat. In the same way a child who has at first filled his pockets with chestnuts will empty them out in order to replace them with the sugared almonds which someone has given him.

Here then we have a comparison of *values*, an *evaluation* of the different objects in the judgements of the savage and the child; but these *evaluations* have nothing fixed about them—they change from one moment to another, as the needs of the person concerned vary. When the savage is hungry, he will set more store by a piece of game than by the best bearskin; but, when his hunger has been satisfied and he is cold, it will be the bearskin which will become precious to him.

Most frequently, the savage confines his desires to the satisfaction of his present needs, and, whatever the quantity in which the objects are available for his use, as soon as he has taken as many of them as are necessary for him he abandons the remainder, which so far as he is concerned are good for nothing.

Experience nevertheless teaches our savage that among the objects suitable for his enjoyment there are some whose nature renders them capable of being kept for some time, and which he may accumulate to meet his future needs: these things retain their *value*, even when the needs of the moment are satisfied. He seeks to appropriate them to himself, that is, to put them in a safe place where he can hide them or defend them. We see that the considerations entering into the estimation of this *value*, which is solely *relative to the man* who is enjoying or desiring, are increased greatly with the advent of this new standpoint, which adds foresight to the primary feeling of need.

It is when this feeling, which was at first only a thing of the moment, assumes a character of permanence, that man begins to compare his needs with one another, and to regulate his search for objects, no longer solely in accordance with the transitory impulse of present needs, but in accordance with the order of the necessity and utility of his different needs.

As to the other considerations by which this order of more or less urgent utilities is balanced or modified, one of the first which presents itself is the excellence of the thing, or its greater or smaller capacity to satisfy the kind of desire which causes it to be sought for. It must be acknowledged that this order of excellence enters to some extent, with respect to the estimation which results from it, into the order of utilities, since the pleasure of the more intense enjoyment which this degree of excellence produces is itself an advantage which a man compares with the more urgent necessity of those things whose abundance he prefers to the excellence of one alone.

A third consideration is the greater or smaller degree of difficulty which a man envisages as being involved in procuring the object of his desires; for it is very obvious that as between two things which possess equal utility and an equal degree of excellence, the one which will take him a great deal of trouble to come by will appear to him to be much more precious, and that he will employ much more care and effort to procure it for himself. It is for this reason that water, in spite of its necessity and the very many pleasures which it procures for men, is never regarded as a precious thing in countries which are well watered, and that men never seek to assure themselves of its possession, since the abundance of this substance enables them to find it ready to hand.

We have not yet arrived at exchange, and here already is *scarcity*, one of the elements of *evaluation*. But it must be said that this esteem which is attached to scarcity is again based on a particular kind of utility, for it is because it is more useful to lay in a stock beforehand of a thing which is difficult to come by that it is more sought after and that men make more effort to appropriate it to themselves.

We can reduce to these three considerations all those which enter into the determination of this kind of value in relation to man in isolation: these are the three elements which combine to form it. In order to give it an appropriate name we shall call it *esteem value* [*valeur estimative*], because it is in actual fact, with complete accuracy, the degree of esteem which man attaches to the different objects of his desires.

It will be worth our while to dwell on this notion, and to analyse what is meant by this degree of esteem which man attaches to the different objects of his desires; what is the nature of this *evaluation*, or the unit term to which the *value* of each object individually is compared; what is the numeration of this scale of comparison; and what is its unit.

If we reflect upon it, we will see that the totality of objects necessary for the maintenance and well-being of man constitutes, if I may use the expression, a *sum of needs* which, in spite of all their extent and variety, is fairly limited.

To provide for the satisfaction of these needs, he has only an even more limited quantity of powers or resources [*facultés*]. Each individual object of his enjoyment costs him trouble, strain, work, and at the very least time. It is this employment of his resources, applied to searching for each object, which constitutes the set-off to his enjoyment and so to speak the *price* of the object. Man is still on his own; nature alone provides for his needs, and already he carries on with her a primary form of *trade*, in which she provides nothing which he does not pay for with his labour, with the employment of his resources and his time.

His capital, in this kind of trade, is confined within narrow boundaries; it is necessary for him to adapt the sum of his enjoyments to it; it is necessary that in the great shop of nature he should make a choice, and that he should apportion this *price* which he has at his disposal among the different objects which answer his purposes, that he should *evaluate* them in proportion to their *importance* for his maintenance and well-being. And what else is this evaluation but the account he renders to himself of the portion of his trouble and his time, or, to express these two words in one alone, of the portion of his resources [*facultés*], which he can employ in the search for the evaluated object without thereby sacrificing the search for other objects of equal or greater importance?

What, then, is his measure of values here? What is his scale of comparison? It is clear that he has no other scale than his resources themselves. The sum total of his resources is the only *unit* of this scale, the only fixed point from which he can start, and the *values* which he attributes to each object are proportional parts of this scale. It follows from this that the *esteem value* of an object, for a man in isolation, is precisely that portion of the total of his resources which corresponds to the desire he has for this object, or that portion which he is willing to employ to satisfy this desire. One might say, putting it in a different way, that it is the relation of this proportional part to the total of the man's resources, a relation which would be expressed by a fraction whose numerator was the unit and whose denominator was the number of values or equal proportional parts which the total resources of the man contained.

We cannot deny ourselves one reflection here. We have still not seen the emergence of trade; we have still not brought two men together; and yet in these very first steps in our investigations we have come within reach of one of the newest and most profound truths which the general theory of value contains. It was this truth which M. the abbé Galiani put forward, twenty years ago, in his treatise *Della Moneta*,[1] with so much clarity and force, but with scarcely any amplification, when he said that *the common measure of all values is man*. It is probable that this same truth, vaguely glimpsed by the author of a work which has just appeared under the title *Analytical Essay on Wealth and Taxation*,[2] gave rise to his doctrine of a constant and unique value always expressed by unity, of which all individual values are only proportional parts—a doctrine which in his version is a mixture of true and false, and which for this reason has appeared somewhat obscure to the majority of his readers.

This is not the place to enlarge upon the elements of obscurity which our readers may in fact find in the short statement we have just given of a proposition which is worthy of being discussed at a length commensurate with its importance; still less, at this moment, should we enter into detail about its numerous consequences.

[1] See above, p. 78, footnote 2. [2] By Graslin (1767).

Let us take up the thread of the argument which has led us to where we now are; let us extend our first assumption. Instead of considering only one man in isolation, let us gather two men together: let each have in his possession certain things suitable for his use, but let these things be different and adapted to different needs. Let us suppose, for example, that two savages land separately on a desert island in the northern seas. One of them brings with him in his boat more fish than he can consume; the other brings more skins than he can use to clothe himself and make himself a tent. The one who has brought fish is cold, and the one who has brought skins is hungry; what will happen is that the latter will ask the possessor of the fish for a part of his supply, and will offer to give him in its place some of his skins: the other will accept. Here we have *exchange;* here we have trade.

Let us stop for a moment to consider what happens in this exchange. It is clear, first, that the man who, after having taken out of his catch the amount necessary for his subsistence for a small number of days beyond which the fish would go bad, would have thrown the remainder away as useless, begins to set store by them when he sees that these fish can serve to procure for him (by way of exchange) the skins which he needs in order to clothe himself; this surplus of fish acquires in his eyes a value which it did not formerly have. The possessor of skins will reason in the same way, and will learn for his part to *evaluate* those for which he does not have a *personal* need. It is probable that in this first situation, where we assume that each of our two men is superabundantly provided with the thing he possesses, and is not accustomed to attach any price to the surplus, the discussion about the conditions of the exchange will not be a very lively one; each will allow the other to take in the one case all the fish and in the other all the skins which he himself does not need. But let us change the assumption a little: let us give to each of these two men an interest in keeping his surplus, a motive for attaching value to it: let us assume that instead of fish one of them has brought maize, which will keep for a very long time; that the other instead of skins has brought firewood; and that the island produces neither corn nor wood. One of our two savages has his subsistence, and the other his heating, for several months; they can go and renew their supplies only by returning to the mainland, from which they have perhaps been driven by the fear of wild beasts or a hostile nation; they can do it only by exposing themselves on the sea, in a stormy season, to almost inevitable dangers. Under these circumstances, it is clear that the total quantity of maize and the total quantity of wood will become very precious to their two possessors, and that they will regard them as having a considerable value; but the wood which the one could consume in a month would become completely useless to him if he died of hunger in the meantime through lack of maize, and the possessor of maize would not be any more advantaged if he were exposed to the risk of dying of cold through lack of wood. Thus they will once again make an exchange, in order that they should both have enough wood and maize to last them until the weather or the season allowed them to go to sea in order to search on the mainland for more maize and more wood. In this situation both will no doubt be less generous; each will very carefully weigh up all the considerations which may induce him to prefer a certain quantity of the good which he does not possess to a certain quantity of that which he does; that is, he will calculate the strength of the two needs, the two interests which he is balancing one against the other—namely, the interest in keeping maize and in acquiring wood, and that in acquiring maize and keeping wood. In a word, he will determine very precisely their *esteem value* relative to himself. This *esteem value* is proportionate to the *interest* which he has in procuring these two things; and the comparison of the two *values* is clearly nothing but the comparison of the two *interests*. But each one makes this calculation separately, and the results may be different: one would exchange three measures of maize for six armfuls[1] of wood; the other would only be willing to give his six armfuls of wood for nine measures of maize. Independently of this kind of mental evaluation in which each man compares the interest which he has in keeping to that which he has in acquiring, both of them are also impelled by an interest which is general and independent of all compari-

---

[1] *Brasses*. A *brasse* is a measure of the distance covered by a man's two outstretched arms. It seems more appropriate, however, to translate it as if Turgot had in fact used the word *brassée*, which is a measure of what a man's two arms can surround and contain.

sons: that is, the interest which each one has in keeping as much as he can of his own good and acquiring as much as he can of the other's good. Having this in view, each one will keep secret the comparison he has inwardly made of his two interests, the two values which he attaches to the two goods which are to be exchanged, and he will sound out the possessor of the good which he desires by making smaller offers and larger demands. The latter will behave for his part in the same way, and they will argue about the conditions of the exchange; and, since they both have a great interest in reaching agreement, they will in the end agree. Little by little, each of them will increase his offers or reduce his demands, until they finally settle that a determinate quantity of maize should be given for a determinate quantity of wood. At the moment when the exchange is made, the one who gives, for example, four measures of maize for five armfuls of wood, no doubt prefers these five armfuls to the four measures of maize; he affords them a higher esteem value; but the one who receives the four measures of maize for his part prefers them to the five armfuls of wood. This superiority of the *esteem value* attributed by the acquirer to the thing which is acquired over the thing which is given up, is essential to exchange, since it is the sole motive for it. Everyone would stay as he was if he did not find an interest, a personal profit, in exchanging—if, relative to himself, he did not esteem what he received more highly than what he gave.

But this difference in esteem value is reciprocal and exactly equal on each side; for, if it were not equal, one of the two would have less desire for the exchange and would force the other to come nearer to his price by means of a higher offer. Thus it is always strictly true that each gives *equal value* in order to receive *equal value*. If four measures of corn are given for five armfuls of wood, then five armfuls of wood are also given for four measures of maize, and consequently four measures of maize *are equivalent*,[1] in this particular exchange, to five armfuls of wood. Thus these two things have an equal *exchange value*.

Let us stop once again. Let us see what exactly is meant by this *exchange value*, the equality of which is the necessary

[1] In French *équivalent*, from the verb *équivaloir* (to be equal in value).

condition of a free exchange; let us not yet depart at all from the simplicity of our hypothesis, in which we have only two contracting parties and two objects of exchange to be considered. It is not exactly the *esteem value*, or, in other words, the interest which each of the two men attached separately to the two objects of need, the possession of which he compared in order to determine what he ought to give up of the one in order to acquire the other, since the result of this comparison could be unequal in the minds of the two contracting parties. This first value, to which we have given the name *esteem value*, is established through the comparison which each of the men separately makes between the two interests which contend with one another in his case; it has no existence except in the mind of each of them taken separately. *Exchange* value, on the other hand, is adopted by both the contracting parties, who acknowledge its equality and make it the condition of the exchange. In the determination of *esteem value*, each man, taken separately, has compared only two interests: the two interests which he attaches to the object which he has and to the object which he desires to have. In the determination of *exchange value*, there are two men who are comparing and there are four interests which are compared; but the two individual interests of each of the two contracting parties have at first been compared with one another separately, and it is the two results which are subsequently compared with one another, or rather argued about, by the two contracting parties, in order to form an *average esteem value* which becomes precisely the *exchange value*, and to which I believe we should give the name *appraisal value* [*valeur appréciative*], because it determines the *price* or the condition of the exchange.

We can see from what has just been said that the *appraisal value*—that value which is equal as between the two objects exchanged—is essentially of the same nature as the *esteem value;* it differs from it only because it is an *average* esteem value. We have seen above that for each of the contracting parties the *esteem value* of the thing which is received is higher than that of the thing which is given,[1] and that this difference is

[1] The original has 'the *esteem value* of the thing which is given is higher than that of the thing which is received', which is obviously an error.

exactly equal on each side; by taking one-half of this difference in order to subtract it from the higher value and add it to the lower, we will make them *equal*. We have seen that this perfect equality is precisely the characteristic of the *appraisal value* of the exchange. This *appraisal value*, therefore, is clearly nothing else but the *average of the esteem values* which the two contracting parties attach to each object.

We have proved that the *esteem value* of an object, for a man in isolation, is nothing else but the relation between the portion of his resources which a man can devote to the search for that object and the totality of his resources; thus the appraisal value in the exchange between two men is the relation between the sum of the portions of their respective resources which they would be disposed to devote to the search for each of the objects exchanged and the sum of the resources of these two men.

It is worth noting here that the introduction of exchange between our two men increases the wealth of both—that is, it gives them a greater quantity of enjoyments with the same resources. Let us assume, in the example of our two savages, that the area which produces the maize and that which produces the wood are far distant from one another. One savage on his own would be obliged to make two voyages to get his supply of maize and his supply of wood; thus he would expend a great deal of time and effort in sailing. If on the other hand there are two of them, they will employ, one in cutting wood and the other in procuring maize, the time and labour which making the second voyage would have involved them in. The sum total of maize and wood gathered in will be greater, and so, consequently, will be the share of each man.

Let us return. It follows from our definition of *appraisal value* that it is definitely not the relation between the two things which are exchanged, or between the *price* and the thing which is sold, as some people have been led to think. The expression 'appraisal value' would be absolutely inappropriate in the comparison of two values, of two terms of exchange. It implies a relation of equality, and this relation of equality presupposes two things which are already equal; but these two things which are equal are definitely not the two things which are exchanged, but rather the values of the things which are exchanged. Thus one should not confuse *values* which have a relation of equality with that relation of equality which assumes two compared values.

There is of course a sense in which *values* have a relation, and we have in fact explained it above when studying the nature of esteem value; we have even said that this relation, like all relations, could be expressed by a fraction. It is precisely the equality between these two fractions which constitutes the essential condition of exchange, an equality which is obtained when the *appraisal value* is fixed at one-half of the difference between the two *esteem values*.

In the language of trade, *price* and *value* are often confused without causing any harm, because a statement of the price always in fact embodies a statement of the value. They are nevertheless different notions, between which it is important to distinguish.

The *price* is the thing which is given in exchange for another thing. From this definition, it clearly follows that this other thing is also the *price* of the first: when we talk about exchange, it is almost superfluous to remark upon this; and since all trade is exchange, it is clear that this expression (the *price*) is always equally applicable to the things which are traded, these being equally the price of one another. The price and the thing which is purchased, or, if you like, the two prices, have an equal value: the price is worth [*vaut*] the thing purchased and the thing purchased is worth [*vaut*] the price; but the word value, strictly speaking, is no more applicable to one of the two terms of the exchange than to the other. Why then do we employ these two terms for one another? Here is the reason, the elaboration of which will enable us to take a further step in the theory of *value*.

The reason is the impossibility of expressing value in terms of itself. One will be readily convinced of this impossibility if one reflects but a moment on what we have stated and proved about the nature of value.

How are we in fact to find the expression of a relation of which the first term, the numerator, the basic unit, is something which cannot be appraised, and which is known only in the vaguest way? How could we decide that the *value* of an object corresponded to a two-fifths part of a man's resources, and of what resources would we be speaking? Certainly we would have to bring into the calculation of these resources the consideration of time, but on what period should we decide? Should we take a whole lifetime, or a year, or a month, or a day? None of these at all, of course; for, relatively to each object of need, the resources of the man, in order to procure these objects, must necessarily be employed during periods of a longer or shorter duration whose inequality is very great. How are we to appraise these periods, when time, while it elapses at once for all the different kinds of needs of the man, ought nevertheless to enter into the calculation only in respect of the *unequal durations* relative to each different kind of need? How are we to evaluate the imaginary parts of a duration which is always one and the same, and which elapses, if I may put it this way, along an indivisible line? And what thread could guide us in such a labyrinth of calculations, in which all the elements are indeterminate? Thus it is impossible to express *value* in terms of itself; and all that human language can state in this respect that the *value* of one thing is equal to the *value* of another. interest which is appraised or rather felt by two men establish this equation in each individual case, without anyone ev having thought of *summing* the resources of the man in order t compare their total with each object of need. Interest always determines the result of this comparison; but it has never made it, nor could it have done so.

Thus the only means of expressing *value*, as we have said, is to state that one thing is equal to another in value; or if you like, putting it in another way, to present one value as equal to the value which is sought for. Value, like extent, has no other measure than value; and we measure values by comparing values with them, just as we measure lengths by applying lengths to them; in both methods of comparison there is no *basic unit* given by nature; there is only an *arbitrary and conventional unit*. Since in every exchange there are two equal values, and since the measure of one can be given by stating the other, it is necessary to agree on the arbitrary unit to be taken as the basis of this measure, or, if you like, as the element of the numeration of the parts of which one's scale of comparison of values is to be composed. Let us suppose that one of the two contracting parties in the exchange wishes to state the value of the thing which he is acquiring: he will take as the unit of his scale of values a constant part of the thing which he is giving, and he will express in numbers and fractions of this unit the quantity of it which he is giving for a fixed quantity of the thing which he is receiving. This quantity will *express* for him *the value* and *will be the price* of the thing which he is receiving; from which we see that *the price is always the expression of the value*, and that therefore, for the acquirer, to *express the value* is to *state the price of the thing* acquired. In stating the quantity of what he gives to acquire it, he will therefore state indifferently that this quantity is *the value* or *the price* of what he is purchasing. In employing these two forms of speech, he will have the same meaning in mind, and will engender the same meaning in the minds of those who hear him; and this brings home the way in which these two words *value* and *price*, although expressing essentially different notions, may be substituted for one another in ordinary language without doing any harm, when we are not seeking to be rigorous and precise.

It is fairly obvious that if one of the two contracting parties has taken a certain arbitrary part of the thing which he gives in order to measure the value of the thing which he acquires, the other contracting party will have the same right in his turn to take this same thing, acquired by his antagonist but given by himself, in order to measure the value of the thing which his antagonist has given to him, and which served as a measure for the latter. In our example, the man who has given four sacks of maize for five armfuls of wood will take as the unit of his scale a sack of maize, and will say: 'An armful of wood is worth [*vaut*] four-fifths of a sack of maize.' The man who has given wood for maize, on the other hand, will take an armful of wood as his unit, and will say: 'A sack of maize is worth one and one-quarter armfuls.' This operation is exactly the same as that which would take place between two men who wanted to evaluate reciprocally, one the French ell in terms of Spanish yards, and the other the Spanish yard in terms of French ells.

In both cases we take, as a fixed and indivisible unit, the thing which is to be evaluated, and we evaluate it by comparing it with a part of the thing which we use for purposes of evaluation, a part which we have arbitrarily taken as the unit. But just as the Spanish yard is no more a measure of the French ell than the French ell is a measure of the Spanish yard, so a sack of maize no more measures the value of an armful of wood than an armful of wood measures the value of a sack of maize.

From this general proposition we may conclude that in *every exchange, each of the two terms of the exchange is equally the measure of the value of the other term*. For the same reason, *in every exchange, the two terms are equally representative pledges of one another*—that is, he who has maize may procure with this maize a quantity of wood of equal value, just as he who has wood may with this wood procure a quantity of maize of equal value.

This is a truth which is extremely simple, but quite fundamental in the theory of value, money, and trade. Completely obvious though it is, it nevertheless often goes unrecognized by men with very good minds, and ignorance of its most immediate consequences has often thrown administrations into the most fatal errors. It is sufficient to cite the famous *System of Law*.[1]

We have dwelt for quite a long time on these first hypotheses of one man in isolation, and of two men exchanging two objects; we have tried to derive from them all the notions of the theory of value which do not require a greater degree of complexity. By always taking our stand in this way on the simplest possible hypothesis, the notions which we show to result from it are necessarily presented to the mind in a clearer and more open manner.

We have only to extend our assumptions, to increase the number of exchangers and of objects of exchange, in order to see the emergence of trade and to complete the series of notions attached to the word *valoir*.

Indeed, it will be sufficient, in order to achieve the latter aim, if we increase the men, never considering any more than two objects of exchange.

If we assume that there are four men instead of two, namely, two possessors of wood and two possessors of maize, we may at first imagine that two exchangers meet one another on one side and two on the other, without any communication between the

[1] The reference is to John Law (1671–1729), the Scottish merchant and financier. The failure of Law's financial operations in France in 1720 was the starting-point for many important discussions on paper money.

four of them; in that case each exchange will be made separately, as if the two contracting parties were alone in the world. But, by virtue of the very fact that the two exchanges are made separately, there is no reason why they should be made on the same conditions. In each exchange taken separately, the *appraisal value* of the two objects exchanged is equal on both sides; but we must not lose sight of the fact that this *appraisal value* is nothing else but the result of the averaging of the two *esteem values* attached to the objects of exchange by the two contracting parties. And it is very possible that the result of this averaging will be completely different in the two exchanges which are separately agreed upon, since the *esteem values* depend upon the way in which each man considers the objects of his needs, and upon the order of utility which he assigns to them among his other needs; they are different for each individual. Consequently, if we consider only two individuals on one side and two individuals on the other, the result of the averaging may be very different. It is very possible that the contracting parties in one of the exchanges will be less sensitive to cold than the contracting parties in the other; this circumstance will be sufficient to cause them to attach less esteem to wood and more to maize. Thus, while in one of the two exchanges four sacks of maize and five armfuls of wood may have an equal *appraisal value*, for the other two contracting parties five armfuls of wood may be equivalent to only two sacks of maize for the other contracting parties[1]—a fact which will not prevent, in each contract, the value of the two objects being exactly equal for the contracting parties, since one is given for the other.

Let us now bring our four men together, and put them in a position to communicate with one another and to acquire knowledge of the conditions offered by each of the proprietors, whether of wood or of maize. As a result of this, the man who has been willing to give four sacks of maize for five armfuls of wood will no longer be prepared to do so if he learns that one of the proprietors of wood is willing to give five armfuls of wood for only two sacks of maize. But the latter, learning in his turn that four sacks of maize can be obtained for the same quantity of five armfuls of wood, will also change his mind, and

---

[1] The last five words are clearly superfluous.

will no longer be prepared to content himself with two. He would be quite prepared to take four; but the proprietors of maize will no more be willing to give them than the proprietors of wood will be willing to content themselves with two. Thus the conditions of the projected exchanges will be altered, and a new *evaluation* will be formed, a new appraisal of the value of maize and the value of wood. It is immediately clear that this appraisal will be the same in the two exchanges and for the four contracting parties, that is, that for the same quantity of wood neither of the two possessors of maize will give either more or less maize than the other, and that conversely the two possessors of wood will not give either more or less wood for the same quantity of maize. We can see at first glance that if one of the possessors of maize demanded less wood than the other for the same quantity of maize, the two possessors of wood would address themselves to him in order to profit from this reduction: this competition would lead the proprietor to demand more wood than he was formerly demanding for the same quantity of maize; the other possessor of maize, for his part, would lower his demand for wood, or raise his offer of maize, in order to attract back to himself the possessors of the wood which he needs; and this process would continue until the two possessors of maize were offering the same quantity of it for the same quantity of wood.

The Marquis de Mirabeau
and François Quesnay

AN EXTRACT FROM

RURAL PHILOSOPHY

(1763)

Source: The text of *Rural Philosophy* from which this translation has been made is that of the three-volume edition stated
to be published in 1764, *A Amsterdam, Chez les Libraires
Associés*, Vol. II, pp. 8–23. The translation is an amended
version of one which was first published in the present editor's
book *The Economics of Physiocracy* (1962), pp. 57–64, and
thanks are due to the publishers of this book, Messrs George
Allen and Unwin, for permission to use it here. All the footnotes
are the present editor's.

François Quesnay (1694–1774), the founder of French Physiocracy, converted the Marquis de Mirabeau (1715–89) to his doctrines at a celebrated interview at Versailles in 1757, and during the next few years the two men collaborated to produce a number of works in which the new Physiocratic ideas were propounded and illustrated. Prominent among these works was the *Philosophie Rurale* (1763), from the eighth chapter of which our next reading has been extracted.

The particular passage I have selected outlines the general theory of 'the origin, the basis, and the form of the different kinds of society' (below, p. 113) which Quesnay seems to have adumbrated in his interview with Mirabeau in 1757,[1] and which constituted the broad sociological framework within which the economic ideas of the Physiocratic school were set. Its importance, however, lies in the fact that its basic notions were adopted not only by the Physiocrats (and Turgot), but also, in one form or another, by the so-called Scottish Historical School, of which Smith was perhaps the most prominent member. Competing 'paradigms'—precisely in order to be able to compete—must have something in common; and one of the most important things which the Physiocratic and Smithian 'paradigms' had in common was this general theory of society.

The extract begins with a remarkable statement of the immensely influential idea that the general shape of society—what Marx was later to call the 'superstructure' of institutions and ideas—depends upon the way in which the society concerned gets its living, or, as Mirabeau and Quesnay put it, upon its 'means of subsistence' (below, p. 104). This section, which bears an interesting resemblance to a passage in Smith's Glasgow lectures,[2] is followed first by a plea to legislators to 'seek in the ways of nature and in the lessons of experience for the most favourable method of enabling the human race to subsist and increase' (p. 107), and then by a striking account of

[1] See R. L. Meek, *The Economics of Physiocracy* (1962), pp. 15–18.
[2] *Lectures on Justice, Police, Revenue and Arms* (ed. E. Cannan, 1896), pp. 159–61.

the progress of society through its main historical stages of development. Three kinds of society in particular are distinguished, in accordance with their different 'modes of life'—hunting, pastoral, and agricultural; and the extract ends with an account of the so-called 'commercial societies' which, it is claimed, are eventually bound to be set up alongside agricultural societies (pp. 108–13).

In the version of this theory presented by Smith and most of the other members of the Scottish Historical School there was one difference of great interest and importance. With Quesnay and Mirabeau, 'commercial societies' are assumed to develop *alongside* agricultural societies, in order to carry on 'mercantile and resale trade' on behalf of the latter. With Smith, by way of contrast, agricultural societies are assumed to develop *into* 'commercial societies'—and these 'commercial societies' are of course of a very different kind from those which Mirabeau and Quesnay had in mind. This difference was a logical consequence of the change of 'paradigm'. But the *general* theory of the development of society was essentially the same, and of the same central significance, in both cases. It is not too much to say that it was this theory, more than any other, which made the further development of a *science* of society possible in the eighteenth century.

RURAL PHILOSOPHY

In order to understand as a statesman the true and simple principles of politics, which is the art of making men useful, and in order to become endowed with a share of that beneficial creative power which produces worthy founders of society or those who add permanent lustre to it, we must consider the common weal in terms of its essence, and humanity as a whole in terms of its root, *subsistence*. All the moral and physical parts of which society is constituted derive from this and are subordinate to it. It is upon subsistence, upon the means of subsistence, that all the branches of the political order depend. Religion, in a sense, is purely and simply spiritual, but natural law inspires us and also tells us about duties relative to our needs; the civil laws, which originally are nothing more than rules for the allocation of subsistence; virtues and vices, which are only obedience to or revolt against natural or civil law; government, the sciences, the liberal and mechanical arts, agriculture, trade, industry—all are subordinate to the means of subsistence. This is the fundamental force to which is due everything which men cultivate, navigate, and build: *quae homines arant, navigant, aedificant, omnia virtuti parent*.[1] If societies endowed with totally different products are seen to be to some extent on a par with one another so far as these aspects of their civil life are concerned, it is solely trade which must be thanked or blamed for this. Trade, which makes products common to all by means of exchange, transplants with the seed the other fruits of society. But imagine yourself suddenly faced with an isolated nation, such as the Lapps and Samoyeds in their snowy abodes are today, or such as the inhabitants of the Island of Newfoundland used to be, confined to fishing for their subsistence; and ask yourself what laws relating to the division of the land, what methods of maintaining the population, what systems of taxation, and what kinds of arts you could get these peoples to accept.

Modern legislators who, without investigating what roots of this kind may exist in the different provinces of a great state, would like to embark upon the destruction of all differences in manners and morals, in laws and customs, and in weights and measures, are self-evidently building on the basis of an illusion. The princes and ministers of former times who sought to enslave nations, either by violence or by corruption, were as foolish as they were barbarous. It is natural that when a society is formed it should want to govern itself: it possesses few types of goods and needs few laws. This is the situation in which all new-born societies find themselves. The whole body of the nation constitutes the magistracy, and the law has no need of assistance: what we have is a republic. This new-born state, which is preoccupied with supplying its needs, is also afraid of very little: it is not yet worth while invading. In order to increase the different kinds of goods it has to increase the number of laws and provide security. Desires are awakened,

[1] 'Success in agriculture, navigation, and building depends invariably on excellence' (Sallust, *Catiline*, ch. 2, para. 7).

each person seeks to acquire gain for himself, and relinquishes his share of the public magistracy. The law requires assistance, and a controlling tutelary power is necessary to guarantee the industrious and prosperous society against invasion. What we have is a legitimate monarchy—though it is often neither very legitimate nor very long-lasting.

The government which wants to secure its authority and preserve it from opposition, then, far from blackening itself by adopting the atrocious and dangerous precautionary policies associated with tyranny, or lowering itself to degrade its people, should seek to make the latter a participant in all the different kinds of goods and all the refinements of products. Consequently it should foresee the dangers of the anarchical authority which is urged upon it by individual interests: I say anarchical, because authority which disrupts the ties binding society together destroys power, and the annihilation of power destroys authority. In the case of everything in this world, abuse is a close neighbour of order. We have just shown the possibilities of the latter. I repeat, change or displace one figure and the whole calculation is thrown into disorder. Introduce one wrong note into the harmony of society, and the whole political mechanism is damaged and falls apart, and concord is then as difficult to re-establish as it would be for the world to take shape as a result of the accidental concourse of atoms of Epicurus.

Thus in dealing here with population, a leading and especially important branch of the speculations of political economy [*la politique économique*], we must look for its principle in its true fountain-head, and set out from the ideas which are really basic in this connection.

Man in this world has only three primary needs: (1) that of his subsistence; (2) that of his preservation; and (3) that of the perpetuation of his species. These three needs are accorded to him, just as they are to all created species, with a degree of urgency depending upon the structure of his organs and the extent of his faculties. Of these three, the first is the only one which is imperative, indispensable, and individual. Numbers of men are unwilling or unable either to defend themselves or reproduce themselves; but no person can live through another. To give up consumption is to give up life. It is to this primary need that we should relate the continuance of humanity, and it is to the means of providing for this need that we should relate the increase of humanity which we call *population*. Subsistence, or expenditure [*dépense*], is therefore at the heart of the matter which we are now discussing, and is the essence of population. Let us seek in the ways of nature and in the lessons of experience for the most favourable method of enabling the human race to subsist and increase.

It is commonly believed that need is the principle of the impulse which we call *desire*. But to hold this opinion is to confuse men with beasts. The only desire of the beast is to satisfy its present appetites, but man has more far-reaching perspectives of welfare, and the satisfaction of his appetites is only, as it were, a diversion from his dominant propensity, which is to desire the enjoyment of full and continual happiness, even if he does not make a very clear distinction between the object of his desire and the aim of his enjoyment. This is the distinctive and superior characteristic of the human species. Those who seek to satisfy this desire through refinements in the satisfaction of their appetites lower themselves deliberately and fruitlessly to the level of the farmyard. The others set themselves aims which are appropriate to their characters, their prepossessions, and their faculties, and which are more or less satisfying according to whether they are more or less free from the fetters of bestiality. From this source have arisen the various idols of our moral passions—freedom, greed, ambition, fame, sensibility, etc.

It is from this point of view that politics ought to fit man into its speculations. Man is compelled to obtain subsistence and induced to obtain enjoyment; and it follows from this that the subsistence which it is least troublesome to obtain is naturally that which suits him best. Thus politics, which is the art of making men useful, and whose first care must be to procure subsistence for them, takes no account of the main motive force of its object if it sets in motion, in order to attain it, nothing but need, and either through ignorance or false principles neglects the most active and flexible spring of action—*desire*. It would then be capable of governing only savages and beasts. The conjunction of these two motive forces, *need* and *desire*, is the principle and the effect of society. The closer they are brought together, the more their driving power is directed towards the same object, and the more tightly-knit and consolidated does society become. The more the ties which bind them together are allowed to be loosened, on the other hand, the more do they part company, and the nearer therefore does society tend towards dissolution.

Such is the point from which we must start if we are to consider, in the light of the true principles of politics, the different forms of society to be found in ancient and modern times, and if we are to acquire sound opinions about the means of enabling them to increase in goods, strength, and population—three things which are indissolubly bound up together in the natural order, the necessary foundation of the political order. Man is compelled by need to seek his food, and induced by desire to procure it and to assure himself of it with the least possible toil and trouble. Such are the contrasting factors which perpetually bring human beings closer to one another, and which perpetually tend to separate them. Such is the source of that monstrous state of affairs in which, when order is subverted, men are almost always at war and engaged in slaughtering one another. This is the light which should guide us from now on in our study of the principles of different societies.

In the beginning, man found himself faced with uninhabited spaces which, in relation to the small number of the first human beings, abounded in goods suitable for subsistence. At first they consumed the spontaneous gifts of nature without making any effort, and enjoyed freedom and idleness, the first objects of desire among uncultured and ignorant peoples. But the fruits of the earth last only for a short time, and do not come back until the following year, whereas man eats every day. He saw population increase, and the means of subsistence become proportionately more troublesome to acquire. Thus it was necessary for him to look for new things on which to subsist. He had to cultivate the land, whence arose agricultural nations. He had to herd together and rear domestic animals, which was the origin of herdsmen. And he had to hunt wild animals and set traps for them, and do the same also for fish, which was the origin of hunters and fishermen.

Of these three modes of life, derived from three different

kinds of subsistence, the first gives rise to settled laws, weights, measures, and everything which is concerned with determining and guaranteeing possessions. It was necessary, before devoting one's toil and sweat to the regular cultivation of a piece of land, to be assured of the possession of the harvest and the enjoyment of its fruits. The second kept innocence and hospitality alive for a longer time, and devoted itself to the sciences, to astronomy, and to speculation. A life which was busy but without strain, abundant but without excess, constrained but without fetters, must have made human nature appear in its best light. Very few laws were needed by men whom nothing tempted to escape from the laws of nature. The third, finally, although the most contemptible and founded on the least secure basis, was in general better adapted to natural licentiousness, to the brutish man. The only laws it could accept were those relating to the gathering together of aggressive forces, the laws of invasion; for the laws of stability are based on the physical extent of the means of subsistence, which in this case were all fortuitous, uncertain, and scattered. By virtue of these same principles, the first of these three kinds of society was settled, the second nomadic, and the third vagrant, piratical, and marauding—always in accordance with the nature and kind of their means of subsistence.

Of these three forms of society, the first could very soon become populous in areas which had to rely on the fertility of the soil to increase the means of subsistence. The second only admitted of a small number of men entrusted with the care of flocks and herds—a small number, that is, in relation to the wide expanse of land required for pasturage. The third could be populous only in proportion to what was obtained in the way of booty; and as it took no care at all to maintain and renew what was provided in this way, it must very quickly have been forced to rush headlong into marauding and to act aggressively against its neighbours, who had united together in industrious or peaceful societies. The most ancient, reliable, and authentic annals of humanity (abstracting from all other ways of looking at them) corroborate the conjectures we have made on the basis of the nature of things. Cain, the first leader of husbandmen, we are told in the scriptures, invented weights and measures. Abraham and Lot, the sons of fellow-herdsmen, virtuous and bound together in friendship, were nevertheless forced to separate from one another, because together they were unable to subsist, increase, and multiply.[1] Nimrod, the first known leader of hunters, was also the first conqueror—a characteristic which can only be a consequence of marauding.

Time and the multiplication of the human species were naturally bound to lead to these different societies intermingling and uniting with one another: to the herdsmen settling down and becoming husbandmen, like the race of Abraham, or scattering out over distant regions, like the Arabs, the Tartars, the primitive nations of the north, and the wandering peoples of America.

Of these nations, those which sooner or later adopted and practised the original art of agriculture have sooner or later come to enjoy the benefits of society, of union, of population, of good and equitable laws, and of the appropriate arts and skills. The others have grown old in a state of barbarism, and have to some extent declined every day in numbers, in skill, and in resources of all kinds.

I say that these different kinds of society intermingled and united with one another, because it was in fact necessary, in order to make a society complete, that it should accept and absorb the seeds and characteristics of each of these original kinds. Agriculture constituted the foundation, but the rearing of livestock became necessary in order to link the plains with the mountains, the pastures with the crops, and the grasslands with cultivation. The art of war, which became necessary for the society to take up in order to ensure the security of its territory, was soon bound to dominate it, both by the weight of its armies and by the direction and employment of the time it devoted to matters of public concern, while each individual busied himself with his own affairs. This predomination, necessarily constrained by equitable rules without which it would have led to invasions and the destruction and dispersal of society—this predomination, I say, constituted the basis of the sovereign authority created by the laws. The art of politics, maintained by force, has need of a leader; and government, having become capable of some extension, was naturally bound

[1] Genesis, Chapter 13.

to fall into the hands of one man. From this originates the tutelary monarchy.

From the interrelationships and drawing together of the different societies there is born a new kind of secondary and artificial society, less secure so far as its basis and duration are concerned, less capable of extension, and unable to form a great empire, but nevertheless free, wealthy, and powerful within its narrow boundaries. Such societies, however, are transitory and subject to change, owing to their excesses, to their carelessness, or to the enterprise of their neighbours, since the way in which they are constituted renders them too much exposed to competition. These are commercial societies.

We have said that the division of the land was necessarily the primary law of the formation of agricultural societies. The distinction between thine and mine was here established in relation to the land, which was done only in order to ensure that it should be established in relation to the fruits of the land. The exchange of the surplus of these fruits for the surplus of a neighbour in whose products the society was deficient was a natural consequence of this state of affairs, so that the exchange of goods through trade became the primary tie binding society together. Mercantile and resale trade, although its basis was only secondary in character and dependent upon cultivation, was nevertheless so necessary that it offered an assured means of subsistence. Whenever we speak of means of subsistence we speak of gain, which here consists in the reward due for the service of distributing goods among the nations. Thus alongside the agricultural societies there could be, and were bound to be, set up commercial societies, just as granaries are set up alongside crops. The republican form of government is appropriate to these societies.

The very basis and institution of these societies would contain the seeds of freedom. In reality, the foundation of their subsistence was their industry, their knowledge of routes and of the surpluses and needs of different areas, and the reputation which they acquired because people grew accustomed to finding them always successful and always scrupulous in fulfilling their obligations. All their possessions consisted of scattered and secret securities, a few warehouses, and passive

and active debts,[1] whose true owners are to some extent unknown, since no one knows which of them are paid and which
of them are owing. No wealth which is immaterial or kept in
people's pockets[2] can ever be got hold of by the sovereign
power, and consequently will yield it nothing at all. This is a
truth which should be constantly repeated to the governments
of those agricultural nations which take such pains to school
themselves to become merchants, i.e. to plunder themselves.
The wealthy merchant, trader, banker, etc., will always be a
member of a republic. In whatever place he may live, he will
always enjoy the immunity which is inherent in the scattered
and unknown character of his property, all one can see of which
is the place where business in it is transacted [*le lieu du
comptoir*]. It would be useless for the authorities to try to force
him to fulfil the duties of a subject: they are obliged, in order to
induce him to fit in with their plans, to treat him as master, and
to make it worth his while to contribute voluntarily to the
public revenue. Such is his essential character, and such
indeed it is important that it should be.

Commercial societies, designated by the name of *comptoirs*,[3]
and thus constituted free by nature, but obliged to make for
themselves laws relating to association, warehousing, and
security, continue to have recourse to sovereign power, without
which important cases would never be resolved and the situation of individuals and the public would never be secure. But
this sovereign power is mixed in character, and varies with
changes in the operations from which profit is made, in the
uncertain means of subsistence. This kind of sovereign power
admits of only a small number of fundamental laws, because the
basis of sovereignty is stability, and few things have a stable
character when possessions are of this type. On the other hand
it includes a large number of regulations relating to the internal
economy and civil administration, because everything in this

---

[1] *Dettes passives & actives*—i.e. liabilities, and book-debts ranking
as assets.

[2] *Richesse de tête & de poche.*

[3] A *comptoir* can mean a table or counter on which a merchant counts
his money or displays his wares; a counting-house; a branch of a
commercial house or bank; or a general commercial office which one
country has established in another.

state of affairs is based upon continual activity, which changes according to different circumstances, and it is necessary at every moment to make provision for the decision of cases and to deal in an orderly and methodical way with a multiplicity of events, which is the general object of all legislation. It follows from this that a sovereign power of such a type has no need of a leader, and indeed that it would not be possible for it to rest in the hands of one man. It is necessary that the members of the social body who share in its benefits should themselves have an eye to instructing and assisting the sovereign power: here we have a republic. Such a state, moreover, does not have a continual need for military forces. Helpful to its neighbours and engaged in serving them, it civilizes them in making them wealthy, or rather in conferring the attribute of wealth on their goods. It is rather from its own arrogance, the child of prosperity, that it has everything to fear. If it alters its character, and exalts itself to the height of its ambition, it will perish, either as a result of its success which will soon cause it to discover a leader in its midst, or as a result of the interruption or evasion of its trade, or as a result of reverses which reduce it to a province of some neighbouring state—which so reduce, that is, its small maritime territory, for so far as its trade is concerned it escapes and will always escape conquest and oppression, through the flight and emigration of those men whose wealth is scattered over different countries. Thus the more peaceful, energetic, and parsimonious these precariously-placed nations are in their prosperity, the more useful and worthy of commendation will they be so far as the agricultural states which border upon them are concerned, and the more it will be in the interests of the latter, when well governed, to favour and support them.

Such is the origin, the basis, and the form of the different kinds of society.

The Marquis de Mirabeau

SIX EXTRACTS FROM
THE *TABLEAU ÉCONOMIQUE* AND
ITS EXPLANATION
(1760)

Source: The text from which the extracts have been translated is that contained in Volume VII (1760) of Mirabeau's *L'Ami des Hommes*. This volume, comprising the Sixth Part of *L'Ami des Hommes*, contains Mirabeau's *Réponse à la Voierie* as well as his *Tableau Oeconomique avec ses Explications*, the pagination for each of these works being separate. The detailed page references for the six extracts are, in order, 15–22, 23–30, 30–40, 41–50, 101–6, and 119–26. The first two-thirds of the Introduction, the last two-thirds of Part Two, Section One, and the last one-third of Part Two, Section Two, have been omitted. Sections One, Two and Three of Part One have been translated in their entirety. Mirabeau's footnotes are keyed in either by asterisks or by lower case italic letters in brackets, and the present editor's by numerical indicators.

We have already met the Marquis de Mirabeau as one of the authors of the last reading. Here we meet him again as the author of a slightly earlier work—his celebrated popularization and elaboration of the ideas of Quesnay's *Tableau Économique*. Quesnay formulated his first version of the *Tableau Économique* in 1758, for the purpose, as he put it in a letter to Mirabeau at the time, of 'displaying expenditure and products in a way which is easy to grasp, and . . . forming a clear opinion about the organization and disorganization [*des arrangements et des dérangements*] which the government can bring about'.[1] In the form which it had assumed by about the end of 1759, when it was distributed by Quesnay to a number of selected individuals, the *Tableau Économique* consisted of an engraved 'zig-zag' diagram; an 'Explanation' twelve pages long; and a set of twenty-four maxims, with extensive notes, under the curious title 'Extract from the Royal Economic Maxims of M. de Sully'.[2]

What the *Tableau Économique* did, in essence, was to explain and illustrate the circular flow of real and money income between the three basic socio-economic classes which were distinguished in the Physiocratic system—the proprietors of land (including the Crown and the Church), the 'productive' class (i.e. all those who worked in agriculture), and the 'sterile' or 'unproductive' class (i.e. all those who worked in manufacture and trade)—on the assumption, central to Physiocracy, that agriculture was the only occupation which was inherently capable of producing a disposable surplus over necessary cost. A diagram was drawn to illustrate the nature, direction, and level of the income flows in a 'state of prosperity' in which all the policies advocated by the Physiocrats were assumed to have been put into operation. This assumption was then removed, and the deleterious effect of the introduction of alternative

[1] R. L. Meek, *The Economics of Physiocracy* (1962), p. 108.
[2] This so-called 'third edition' of the *Tableau* is reproduced in facsimile, with an English translation, in *Quesnay's Tableau Économique* (ed. M. Kuczynski and R. L. Meek, 1972).

policies was analysed in terms of the successive alterations to the original income flows which it would induce. In Quesnay's early formulations of 1758–9 this analysis was entirely verbal; in later formulations further diagrams were drawn to illustrate these '*dérangements*'.

The ingenuity of Quesnay's attempt was breathtaking: the only trouble was that his 1758–9 formulations of the *Tableau* were so condensed, disorderly, and enigmatic that nobody could really understand what he was getting at. Mirabeau, therefore, in co-operation with Quesnay, immediately set about the task of popularization and the result was the lengthy 'Explanation' of the *Tableau* which he published in 1760 in the sixth (and last) part of his famous book *L'Ami des Hommes*. What Mirabeau did in this 'Explanation' was in essence a job of re-organization, clarification, and expansion. Something like five-sixths of the original material in the version of the *Tableau* which Quesnay distributed in 1759 reappears in the 'Explanation', but its order and arrangement are completely altered; there is a logical division into two main parts (dealing respectively with the '*arrangements*' and the '*dérangements*') with seven chapters in each; there are six diagrams instead of one; and a great deal of new textual material has been added by Mirabeau himself—which accounts for the odd mixture of styles which discerning readers will detect in our extracts.

The first of the extracts (below, pp. 120–3) consists of the final part of Mirabeau's Introduction, in which a number of fundamental Physiocratic concepts and presuppositions are fairly clearly set out. The second, third, and fourth extracts (pp. 123–38) are concerned with the explanation of the basic diagram in the assumed 'state of prosperity'· The reader will find, I think, if he can reconcile himself to the cumbersome 'zig-zag' method of depicting the income flows,[1] and if he can forget about the various problems which are bypassed,[2] that Mirabeau's explanation is sufficiently clear to render any further explanation by the present editor unnecessary at this juncture. There are, however, a number of questions relating

[1] This method was abandoned by Quesnay and Mirabeau in most of their subsequent formulations.

[2] Most notably, that of where the sterile class gets its own manufactured goods from!

to some of the terminology used, and to some of the arith-metical calculations, which I have dealt with in footnotes to my translation of Mirabeau's text.

The last two extracts (below, pp. 138–46), dealing with the '*dérangements*', are interesting exercises in what we might call today dynamic welfare economics. In the first, it is assumed that 'the *Tableau* has lost its equilibrium' (p. 139) because the landlords, and, following them in good Cantillonian fashion the other social classes, have increased their propensity to con-sume manufactured goods. In the second, it is assumed that the *Tableau* has lost its former 'complete immunity' (p. 144) because of the imposition of a tax which falls on agricultural capital. Each of these departures from the Physiocratic policy norms, it is argued, will lead to a cumulative decline in the level of income and economic activity. The political moral of these fascinating pieces of analysis would not have been lost on the readers of 1760: if the present level of income in France is in fact far lower than the level assumed in the original 'state of prosperity' diagram, the reason for this can only be that '*dérangements*' such as those described in these two chapters are now actually occurring.

The comments in the *Wealth of Nations* on Physiocracy in general and the *Tableau Économique* in particular are very interesting.[1] To Smith, of course, the 'capital error' of the Physiocratic system lay 'in its representing the class of artificers, manufacturers and merchants, as altogether barren and unproductive'[2]—a notion which was indeed quite irrecon-cilable with his own 'paradigm', and which he vigorously attacked. The curious thing, however, is that in his description of the Physiocratic system Smith makes it appear as if the Physiocrats assumed that both agriculture *and manufacture* were normally carried on under the direction of capitalists who employed wage-labour, and that the income of all these capital-ists normally consisted of profit at the 'ordinary rate' on their capital. These assumptions are of course clearly made in Smith's own system, and up to a point in the system of Tur-got's *Réflexions;* but they were *not* clearly made in any of the 'official' Physiocratic works of the time.

[1] *Wealth of Nations* (ed. E. Cannan, 6th edn., 1950), Vol. II, pp. 182–200.
[2] ibid., Vol. II, p. 119.

So far as the *Tableau Économique* is concerned, Smith was obviously worried about the fact that it embodied the 'capital error' of the system, and he no doubt felt that the problem of the general interdependence of the elements of the economic universe was too important and too complex to be dealt with within the framework of a simple schematic diagram. But the main complaint which he actually voices about the *Tableau*, significantly enough, concerns the analysis of the '*dérangements*'. Why, he asks in effect, should it be assumed that the economic system is so feeble that even quite small divergences from the ideal regime will cause it not merely to stop advancing, but actually to go backwards? Just as the human body contains within itself 'some unknown principle of preservation, capable either of preventing or of correcting in many respects, the bad effects even of a very faulty regimen', so in the political body 'the natural effort which every man is continually making to better his own condition, is a principle of preservation capable of preventing and correcting, in many respects, the bad effects of a political œconomy, in some degree both partial and oppressive'.[1] This belief in the innate capacity of the economic system to continue advancing 'towards wealth and prosperity' in the face of all but the most formidable obstacles, and to readjust itself in the face of all but the most severe shocks, was an important ingredient of the new Smithian 'paradigm'. We shall come across the same point again in the introduction to the extracts from Steuart's *Inquiry*.

THE *TABLEAU ÉCONOMIQUE* AND ITS EXPLANATION

From the Introduction

... One might, before beginning [to study the *Tableau*], frame certain basic preliminary notions, such as, for example:

The land is the mother of all goods.

Among these goods, all those which are consumed by the man

---

[1] ibid., Vol. II, pp. 194–5.

who cultivates the land constitute subsistence; it is only those which he is able to sell which may constitute wealth.

If a man cultivates the land with his hands, he will derive from it only his subsistence and that of his family, and will indeed live very poorly. Thus he must find a form of assistance which will furnish him with a larger product, and demand less from him by way of upkeep.

This assistance consists of machines, livestock, wheat,[1] manure, etc. All these things have prices, the total of which makes up the mass of the original advances [*avances primitives*].

As these things are consumed and worn away when put to work, they require upkeep and repairs, the total amount of which, together with the costs of consumption of those who put them into operation, and the seed, etc., constitutes what we call the annual advances [*avances annuelles*], since every year one must repair and replenish one's workshops, live, work and sow before gathering anything in.

The fruit of good cultivation ought to be an ample harvest which provides for (1) the return of the annual advances, in anticipation of and preparation for the future harvest; (2) interest on the original advances, that is, an honest profit, which serves as a revenue from the funds employed in machines, livestock, manure, etc.; and (3) the gain of a surplus product, which the cultivator may sell or exchange.

It is this surplus which we call revenue. It alone is wealth, because it is the only disposable portion; all the remainder is necessarily devoted to the indispensable maintenance of the working parts of the economic machine.

Upon this portion which we have established as *wealth* and called *revenue*, the whole economic structure turns. It is from this portion that there are deducted (1) the tithes allotted to the upkeep of the churches and the other services of religion; and (2) the public revenue assigned to the support and defence of society. The remainder forms what we call the revenue of the proprietors, that is, the rent of the land whose cultivation is handed over to the enterprise of the cultivators, and for which they render such-and-such an amount to the proprietor, free and quit of the costs of cultivation.

[1] *Foment* in the original text, which I have taken to be a misprint of *froment*.

Of these three portions, the first directly supports all who are committed to the service of religion; the second all who are hired for the service of the public; and the third all who are employed in the service of the proprietors.

The three together, and each of them separately, maintain indirectly, and by the dictate of necessity, the whole of the working section of the nation, the cultivators as well as the manufacturing workers; so that these men, who up to harvest-time have lived only on their advances, then live on the *revenue*, which is paid back to them in order to buy their surplus, and which provides them with the means of paying in their turn those who have for sale a surplus of the things which they lack and which they have not harvested or manufactured.

Here we have the whole machinery of circulation, represented here in terms of the stock of money, which is itself not subsistence but a facility for the exchanges that are customary among all peoples.

It is this circulation which is delineated in the *Tableau* we are going to present, and the explanation of which is to be studied.

We shall see from this that by means of the circulation between the three classes, namely, the class of proprietors, the productive class, and the hired or working class, the total which circulates would appear to be double the real total constituted by the advances.

But we must perceive clearly the physical aspect of wealth—i.e. its reproduction, without which no one could live for more than a year.

We shall then see that wealth has only one source, namely, the productive class, which sets in motion all the others, providing them with means which return to the productive class doubled, through the favourable stimulus of an abundant, well-conducted, and regular circulation.

It is this which must be considered in the *Tableau*. The fourteen subdivisions which it contains, which look as if they were successive [*graduelles*], are in fact merely distributive; and it is in one and the same year that the whole of this allocation is carried out, with all the infinite ramifications which society involves.

Moreover, we have by no means set out to make of it an

algebraic work, considered in all the connections of which it is capable. That would amuse a geometrician, but would not conduce at all to the object of the author, who has presented in the *Tableau* only those aspects which are absolutely necessary; and such as it is, one will still find it only too complicated.

The understanding of the *Tableau* will lead to an understanding of the depredations to which it is assumed that circulation may become subject; and everyone who takes the trouble necessary to possess himself of all the principles which spring from this economic study will be recompensed for his labour by the certitude of the results and by the prescience he will have acquired concerning the nature and effects of all political processes.

So far as the arithmetic is concerned, we know that in matters of reasoning *errors excepted* is always taken to be appended to arithmetical calculations. The truths which are embodied in the *Tableau* do not depend on the degree of greater or less which these hieroglyphics called figures represent. The diagrams of the *Tableau*, which will at first appear to be the most complicated part of the work, have been put in only in order to facilitate the comprehension of the latter. One must speak to the eyes, in support of the language appropriate to the understanding. The latter is liable to relax, and mechanical matters summon back its attention. Finally, everywhere else the demonstrator is ready to agree, when he is not understood, that it is his own fault, but here it will be the fault of a lack of application on the part of the reader.

PART ONE, SECTION ONE

The Tableau Économique
Considered in Connection with its Construction

It is first necessary to deal with the question of where the revenue comes from, how it is distributed between the different classes of society, in what places it gets lost, and in what places it is reproduced.

For this purpose the author draws up three columns. That on

TABLEAU ŒCONOMIQUE.

OBJETS à considérer : 1°. *trois sortes de depenses ;* 2°. *leur source ;* 3°. *leurs avances ,* 4°. *leur distribution ;* 5°. *leurs effets ,* 6°. *leur réproduction ;* 7°. *leurs rapports entr'elles ,* 8°. *leurs rapports avec la population ,* 9°. *avec l'Agriculture ,* 10°. *avec l'industrie ,* 11°. *avec le commerce ,* 12°. *avec la masse des richesses d'une Nation.*

DÉPENSES PRODUCTIVES relatives à l'Agriculture, &c.	DEPENSES DU REVENU, l'Impôt prélevé, se partagent aux dépenses productives & aux dépenses stériles.	DÉPENSES STÉRILES relatives à l'industrie, &c.

AVANCES ANNUELLES pour produire un revenu de 600 liv. sont 600 liv.	REVENU annuel de	AVANCES ANNUELLES pour les Ouvrages des dépenses stériles sont
600ᵗᵗ produisent net..................600ᵗᵗ		300ᵗᵗ
PRODUCTIONS.		OUVRAGES, &c.

300ᵗᵗ reproduisent net..................300ᵗᵗ...................300ᵗᵗ

250ᵗ reproduisent net..................150ᵗ...................150ᵗ

75ᶠ reproduisent net..................75ᵗ...................75ᶠ

37. 10 ſ. reproduisent net..........37. 10. ſ...................37. 10.ſᵒ

18. 15ſ reproduisent net..........18. 15ᵒ...................18. 15ᵒ

9. 7. 6 d. reproduisent net......9. 7. 6. d....................9. 7. 6.dᵒ

4. 13. 9 reproduisent net..........4. 13. 9....................4. 13. 9ᵒ

2. 6. 10 reproduisent net..........2. 6. 10....................2. 6. 10ᵒ

1. 3. 5 reproduisent net..........1. 3. 5....................1. 3. 5ᵒ

0. 11. 8 reproduisent net..........0. 11. 8....................0. 11. 8ᵒ

0. 5. 10 reproduisent net..........0. 5. 10....................0. 5. 10ᵒ

0. 2. 11 reproduisent net..........0. 2. 11....................0. 2. 11ᵒ

0. 1. 5 reproduisent net..........0. 1. 5....................0. 1. 5ᵒ

&c.

REPRODUIT TOTAL ...... 600. *liv.* de revenu. De plus les frais annuels de 600. *liv.* & les intérêts des avances annuelles & des avances primitives du Laboureur, de 345 *liv.* que la terre restitue. Ainsi la reproduction est de 1545 *liv.* compris le revenu de 600. *livres*, qui est la base du calcul, abstraction faite de l'Impôt de 300. *liv.* de la dixme de 150. *liv.* des avances & des intérêts de ces avances, & des avances primitives qu'exige sa reproduction annuelle, *&c.* Toutes ces parties réunies formeroient ensemble une réproduction totale de 2705 *liv.* ce qui est en bonne culture, la moitié du produit de l'emploi d'une charruë, comme il sera expliqué ci-après.

The *Tableau* to which Sections One, Two and Three of Part One of Mirabeau's explanation refer.

the left[1] comprises productive expenditure, i.e. agriculture. That on the right[2] comprises sterile or manufacturing expenditure. In the middle is the column showing the revenue, whose payment back to the just and the unjust alike puts the whole machinery of circulation in motion, sets on foot the movement of society, and gives pith and marrow to its subsistence.

The author takes as an example a revenue of 600 livres,[3] considered here separately from taxes and tithes so as not to complicate the figures unduly; and these 600 livres can be understood, if one wishes, as 600 million.

The kingdom taken here is one in a good state of cultivation, where the reproductive expenditure renews the same revenue from year to year; that is, where agriculture yields, all kinds of product being taken together, 100 per cent of the annual costs which are devoted to it; where an acre[4] of land brings in every year on the average 10 livres of revenue for the proprietor, 5 livres for taxes, and 2 livres 10 sous for tithes, making a total of 17 livres 10 sous, together with as much again for the restitution of the advances and 10 livres for the interest on these advances; where an acre must consequently bring in annually at least 45 livres. The year in which it bears the harvest of wheat must produce double this amount per acre, because of the fallow year which precedes it and which brings it about that this harvest combines together two years. Thus on the hypothesis of a net product of 100 per cent, this harvest must amount to at least 90 livres per acre, and the harvest of spring corn to 45 livres per acre. But wheat requires proportionately much greater costs than spring corn, and yields proportionately much more; thus the product of an acre of wheat should be estimated at 110 livres, and that of an acre of spring corn at 25 livres, which amounts to the same thing in the aggregate.

Our hypothesis excludes small-scale cultivation [*la petite culture*] carried on with the aid of oxen, etc. This kind of work,

---

[1] The original text has 'right' [*droite*], an obvious error.
[2] The original text has 'left' [*gauche*], again an obvious error.
[3] The *livre* contained twenty *sols* (=*sous*), each of which contained twelve *deniers*.
[4] *Arpent*—the French acre, equal to about one and a quarter English acres.

to which cultivators are reduced owing to their lack of the funds necessary to make the original advances which cultivation demands, is carried on only at the expense of landed property itself. The hay on the grasslands is consumed by the oxen; a large part of the land is employed as pasture and for other uses, left lying fallow, waste, etc., on the pretext of allowing it to rest—in a word, it is eaten up by costs. This work, I say, requires an excessive annual expenditure for the subsistence of the great numbers of men engaged in this type of cultivation, and this expenditure absorbs almost the whole of the product. This thankless type of cultivation, which reveals the poverty and ruin of those nations in which it predominates, has no connection with the order of our *Tableau*, where we assume a situation in which the annual advances are able, with the aid of the fund of original advances, to produce 100 per cent.

This also assumes that the market value of corn is at the level which should be maintained by means of free and unobstructed internal and external trade, that is, that the price of wheat is at least equal to the value of one-third of a silver mark, or to 18 livres of our present money, per Paris septier.[1] This condition should be taken to be implied throughout; for without an estimation of the actual price of the produce of the soil one cannot acquire any idea of the situation regarding the expenditure, the products, or the revenue of a nation. Let us now describe in detail what is meant here by the two expressions *original advances* and *annual advances*.

The *original advances*, which have not been incorporated in the *Tableau* presented here lest it should become too complicated, are the initial funds which it is necessary to lay out on a farm whose exploitation one wishes to undertake. In many places people are too unaware, and are forced by poverty to be unaware, of the enormous advantages which arise from sparing nothing so far as this type of advances is concerned. The land is a grateful mother, who returns with interest what is lent to her, and this in an infinite progression for us. But in relation to the hypothesis adopted in the *Tableau*, we may postulate that the full total of the original advances required for putting a

---

[1] A Paris *septier* (=*setier*) of corn was about twelve bushels.

plough of land[1] under large-scale cultivation [*la grande culture*] is estimated at 10,000 livres for the first fund of expenditure on livestock, implements, fodder, seed and food, upkeep, wages, etc., in the course of the two years' preparatory work which we must assume precedes the first harvest.

It is this fund of original advances, the necessity and importance of which make themselves felt through the very word 'advances',[2] which must above all be attended to in an agricultural state. One hears it said among the blind or the guilty: 'But for the last twenty years the talk has always been of poverty, and yet the people pay, and moneys due are collected.' If in ploughing their land men are driven to descending from large horses to medium-sized ones, from these to ponies, and from the latter to mules, asses, etc., then it is possible that for a period the people will pay in this way out of their capital [*fonds*]; and the inevitable ruin which this represents at the time becomes irreparable later.

The *annual advances* are the funds employed each year in the preparation of a product. They include two things—on the one hand the annual productive expenditure, and on the other hand the annual sterile expenditure.

The annual *productive expenditure* is employed in agriculture, on grasslands, pastures, forests, mines, fishing, and the food and other necessities of the men engaged in the work of this class, etc., in order to perpetuate wealth in the form of corn, drink, wood, livestock, raw materials for manufactures, etc.

The annual *sterile expenditure* is on manufactured commodities, house-room, clothing, interest on money, servants, commercial costs, foreign products, wages of workers, etc.

The author, by fixing his postulated total of revenue at 600 livres, and by assuming that its production is based on a yield of 100 per cent in cultivation, consequently brings out the total

[1] Literally, 'for the establishment of one plough'. Mirabeau, like Quesnay in the original *Tableau*, would seem to be using the word *charrue* (plough) to mean a plough *of land* (a carucate or ploughland), this being a measure of the amount of land that can be tilled with one plough in a year.

[2] Literally, 'at the first word which denotes them'—i.e. presumably, the first of the two words in '*avances primitives*', the expression which I have translated as 'original advances'.

of the annual advances or productive expenditure at 600 livres. On the same hypothesis, by postulating an expenditure proportionate to the revenue in the field of industry, he determines the annual advances for the annual sterile expenditure at 300 livres. Let us now examine the progression [*marche*] of the revenue and that of the circulation, in accordance with this assumed order of things.

PART ONE, SECTION TWO

The Tableau Économique
Considered in Connection with its Progression*

The annual advances of 600 livres devoted to the land by the cultivator bring him in a net product of 600 livres for the proprietor.

This hypothesis will appear fictitious to so many poor proprietors who are too pleased at finding those wretched cultivators called *métayers*,[1] with whom they share the fruits of all kinds. So deficient a form of cultivation cannot support such conditions, moreover, since at the slightest calamity the master has to feed the *métayer*, or the latter will do a moonlight flit. But this deplorable form of cultivation, daughter of necessity and mother of poverty, has nothing in common with good cultivation [*la bonne culture*], such as is established in certain countries and is assumed here, where the farmer, independent so far as his food is concerned, receives from the master nothing but the groundwork of the product, and even has his own fund of original advances, on which the land pays him interest of at least ten per cent. This part of the annual returns of the farmer, as I have said above, has not been included in the *Tableau* at all; but the author includes it, giving a figure of 345 livres for

---

* See the *Tableau* on p. 124.

[1] *Métayage* is a system of tenure in which the cultivator (the *métayer*) pays part of the product as rent to the proprietor, who furnishes the stock, seed, etc.

it, in the summary at the foot of the *Tableau* for the part relative to the revenue of 600 livres.[1] Let us proceed.

The annual advances of 300 livres assumed here for the sterile expenditure class are employed for the capital [*fonds*] and costs of trade, for the purchase of raw materials for manufactured goods, and for the subsistence and other needs of the artisan until he has completed and sold his work. But they do not reproduce anything, as everyone knows, and as can be seen in the *Tableau*. Industry, I say, produces nothing, and gives in all cases only a relative increase in value.

Of the 600 livres of net product which form the revenue of the proprietor, one-half is spent by the latter in purchasing bread, wine, meat, etc., from the productive expenditure class, and the other half in purchasing clothing, furnishings, utensils, etc., from the sterile expenditure class.

The portion of the revenue amounting to 300 livres which according to the order of the *Tableau* passes at first into the hands of the productive expenditure class, represents *advances* of that amount which are returned in the form of money, and which in the course of the year reproduce 300 livres net, which represents the reproduction of part of the proprietor's revenue for the following year; and it is by means of the remainder of the distribution of the sums of money which are returned in the same year to this same class, as we see happening stage by stage in the *Tableau*, that the total revenue is reproduced each year.

These 300 livres, I say, which the proprietor has paid back to

[1] The figure of 345 livres in the summary at the foot of the *Tableau* on p. 124 is in fact there stated to be for the interest on the original *and annual* advances of the husbandman. The way in which this figure of 345 livres is derived will not be immediately apparent. The starting-point would seem to be the *Tableau* on p. 137, in which taxes and tithes (amounting together to 450 livres) are *not* abstracted from, so that the total 'revenue' is not 600 but 1050 livres. In this situation, the annual advances of the husbandman will also be 1050 livres, on which he will receive interest at 10%—i.e. 105 livres. In addition, he will receive interest at 10% on one-half of the original advances required for 'the establishment of one plough'—i.e. 10% on 5,000 livres, which amounts to 500 livres. Thus his total receipts in the form of interest, when the 'revenue' is 1050 livres, are 605 livres. When the 'revenue' is only 600 livres, as it is assumed to be in the *Tableau* on p. 124, Mirabeau apparently assumes that the receipts in the form of interest will be scaled down proportionately—i.e. that they will $\frac{600}{1050}$ of 605 livres, which works out at 345 livres.

the productive expenditure class, are spent by the farmer, one-half in the consumption of products provided by this class itself—bread, wine, meat, etc.—and one-half on clothing, utensils, tools, etc., provided by the sterile class.

The 300 livres of the proprietor's revenue which have passed into the hands of the sterile expenditure class are spent by the artisan, as to one-half, in the purchase from the productive expenditure class of bread, wine, and meat for his subsistence, or of raw materials for his work, and for foreign trade. The other half is distributed among the sterile expenditure class itself for its maintenance, and for the restitution of its advances, that is, of that sum above-mentioned which is advanced by the artisan until he has completed and sold his work.

This circulation and mutual annual distribution are continued in the same way by means of subdivisions down to the last denier of the sums of money which mutually pass from the hands of one class into those of another. Let us now examine the return and the total of these funds.

We see by adding the sums brought into the sterile expenditure column that circulation brings 600 livres to this class. Of this, 300 livres must first be kept back for the replacement of the *annual advances*. This leaves 300 livres for wages. In this way, it turns out that the 300 livres which at first pass from the hands of the proprietor into those of the sterile expenditure class replace the 300 livres of its annual advances, and that the wages, on the other hand, are paid from the 300 livres which this class receives from the productive expenditure class.

The product of the productive class amounts to 1200 livres, abstracting from taxes, tithes, and interest on the husbandman's advances, items which will be considered separately so as not to complicate the order of expenditure too much. The product, I say, amounts to 1200 livres, namely, 600 livres which we have put into the hands of the proprietor, and 600 livres which constitute the return of the *annual advances* of agriculture. Let us trace out the way in which these 1200 livres are employed.

We have said that the proprietor buys 300 livres' worth of the products of the soil, which amounts to the same thing as if he received half his revenue in the form of products. Three hundred livres' worth passes into the hands of the sterile expenditure class, namely, 150 livres which remain from the first payment of 300 livres made by the proprietor (for we see that as a result of the transfer which the sterile class makes at each stage to the productive class, it retains for itself only one-half of what it has received), and 150 livres which it receives through the various transfers which the productive class makes to it. Of the 600 livres' worth which remain, one-half is consumed within the productive expenditure class by the men who cause the product to be generated, and the product of the other half is employed to complete the payment of the rent to the proprietor.[a]

Each year the advances of the productive class bring about the regeneration of the advances and the revenue; and similarly each year the revenue and these advances are consumed and reproduced. Each year, too, the advances are consumed by the farmer: they are themselves the costs or expenses which he incurs for their reproduction and for the reproduction of the revenue, which is the net product that cultivation brings in over and above the costs. If the advances were too small and reproduced no more than the advances or costs, there would be no one other than the cultivators and those members of the sterile class whose work they bought who would subsist on the products of the land. Thus if any others, i.e. the state, the proprietor, or the tithe-owner, demanded revenue, they would take away the subsistence of the former and destroy the advances which cause it to be generated, and the land would be abandoned: no more cultivation, no more industry, and no more trade.

Thus it is necessary, in order to sustain the opulence, population, and power of a nation, that the farmers' advances should be sufficient to cause the land to yield the greatest possible net product or revenue, through the greatest possible abundance of products and market value. Moreover, it is important for each nation, by means of the market value of the produce of its soil, to maintain itself in that degree of opulence

(a) The fodder for the livestock, although derived from the products of the land, is not brought into the reckoning here, since the sale of livestock itself forms a part of the revenue.

Neither is the reproduction of the 600 livres of advances considered here at all, since they must be employed afresh on the land in order that a harvest may be reaped in the following year.

which is most advantageous relatively to the wealth of neighbouring nations and relatively to the mutual trade which it carries on with them; for it would be very detrimental to it to sell to them at a low price, and to buy what they sold to it at a high price. Such a trade would be wholly to their advantage, and would upset the order of relative wealth as between it and its neighbours. This is what may happen as the result of bad civil administration, of taxes, and of ridiculous regulations which invert the natural order of a nation's trade.

Let us come back to the 300 livres which, on the hypothesis of a net product of 100 per cent, were allotted to the sterile expenditure class, in order to take into consideration external trade, which secures the sale of that portion of the produce of the soil which is in excess of the consumption of an agricultural nation.

Of these 300 livres, one-half, i.e. 150 livres, is consumed for subsistence within this class itself; and the other half, amounting to 150 livres, is taken for external trade, which is included in this same class. Thus one-eighth of the total product enters into external trade as exports, and as raw materials and subsistence for those of the country's workers who sell their work to other nations. The traffic which is called mutual foreign trade consists in the fact that the sales of the merchant counterbalance the purchases of the commodities and bullion which are obtained from other nations.

Such is the order of the distribution and consumption of the products of the soil as between all the classes of citizens; and such is the view which we ought to take of the use and extent of external trade in a flourishing agricultural nation, where the government puts no obstacles at all in the way of trade in the produce of the soil. Thus in a nation where the territory produced every year 2 milliards 400 millions, the sales of products abroad would amount to 300 millions. This is the true trade of a well-governed agricultural nation, the trade which is appropriate for it. It is this trade which maintains the sales and market value of the produce of the soil, which makes agriculture flourish, which results in the development of all the land, which assures the revenue of the sovereign and the proprietors, and which procures gains for the men employed in the sterile expenditure class.

PART ONE, SECTION THREE

The Tableau Économique
Considered Relatively to Population *

Mutual sales from one expenditure class to the other distribute to both sides the revenue of 600 livres, giving 300 livres to each.

The proprietor subsists by means of the 600 livres which he spends. The 300 livres which he distributes to each class, together with the product of the taxes, the tithes, etc., which is added to them, can support one man in each class; thus 600 livres of revenue together with their appurtenant sums can enable three heads of families to subsist.

On this basis 600 millions of revenue can enable three million families to live, estimated at four persons of all ages per family.

We have said that the annual advances of the productive class, which are nothing but the costs incurred for the purposes of reproduction, are regenerated each year. We have said that one-half, i.e. 300 livres, serves to pay the wages of the men whom the farmer employs in the work of production. These 300 livres maintain another head of family, and since these 300 livres stand for 300 millions, that means another one million heads of families.

Thus these 900 millions, which, abstracting from taxes, tithes, and interest on all advances both original and annual, would be annually regenerated from landed property, could enable sixteen million people of all ages to subsist, according to this order of circulation and distribution of the product and the annual revenue.

By circulation is here meant only the purchases at first hand paid for by the revenue which is shared out among all classes of men, abstracting from trade, which multiplies sales and purchases without multiplying things, and which represents nothing but an addition to sterile expenditure. Thus we see simply from a glance at the *Tableau* that the sum of money

* See the *Tableau* on p. 124.

representing the annual revenue of landed property is sufficient for circulation in the trade of an agricultural nation.

Here, then, we have sixteen million people living in a state where the proprietors have a revenue of 600 millions. But so far we have abstracted from taxes and tithes, which, when added to the proprietors' revenue, ought to enable these sixteen million people to live in easy circumstances, if the population is limited to this number, which would be in the proportion most conducive to the prosperity of the state; for the wealthier is the agriculture of a nation, the less men it employs in the cultivation of corn, and the more it has need of export trade in order to maintain the abundance and market value of its products. Every flourishing nation, in order to enjoy its annual wealth, needs to buy from abroad the commodities which it does not itself produce. Thus it is necessary for it to counterbalance these purchases with its sales abroad of a surplus of its own products. Without this mutual trade its wealth would waste away, and its products would have no fixed and constant price. The annual returns of the husbandman would never be assured; the revenue of the sovereign and the proprietors would decline; and the population maintained by the revenue would diminish.

Industry and manufactures do not constitute, through their sales abroad, an assured means of maintaining the population of a kingdom. They may be set up anywhere, to the extent that need and profit may attract them; they are impermanent and inconstant. A nation has no true source of wealth other than the extent and fertility of its soil. An agricultural kingdom ought to rely on nothing but a population maintained in easy circumstances through the wealth which it derives from its territory; such a population can cope with all the uses to which the territory may be put, in conformity with the state of its wealth.

In calculating how many inhabitants living in reasonable comfort this or that amount of revenue can maintain, we do not mean either to set any limits to, or to calculate, the infinite number of midges which live round about a flourishing hive—midges which have no absolute assurance of subsistence, but which are nevertheless maintained by the voluntary retrenchments of the others, and by their own economy and willingness meekly to content themselves with the scraps thrown away by them. If in coming into my house I see a kitchen-boy with his two feet held by two small stool-carriers, this transaction does not imply that in the emoluments and honoraria of his employment I have laid down so much for his boot-blacks; but as soon as he thinks fit to spend money on them out of his slender wages, he has his good or bad reasons which, when coupled with a host of similar good or bad reasons, enable a large number of those over-obliging and parsimonious midges called Savoyards to live. Thus it is that above and beyond the number of inhabitants whose subsistence is assured in a large state, the population is necessarily augmented by a large number of other chance-comers who are attracted by the smell of the cooking-pot and live on the scum. This section of the population, however, is always relative to the product and dependent upon it; and if the product happens to decline, it is with good reason the first to be destroyed.

We shall see presently[1] how and why it is necessary to reckon taxes in addition as one-half of the revenue of the proprietors. Thus where the proprietors have a revenue of 600 millions, taxes ought to amount to 300 millions,[a] and tithes to 150 millions. These two additions form a total of 450 millions. This sum, since it is an annual revenue which is distributed in the same way as the revenue of the proprietors, should be divided out among the same number of heads in the form of subsistence and improvements in well-being.

The return of the annual advances in respect of these two new parts of the revenue, brought under the same rule which we have deduced above for the return of the annual advances relative to the revenue of the proprietors, makes an additional total of 225 millions which is included in the distribution extending to all classes of citizens.[2]

---

[1] In Part One, Section Four, which is not included in these extracts.

[a] These 300 millions of taxes, paid by landed property, are raised without any costs or charges either on men or on commodities. France, if well cultivated, could provide in the same way taxes of more than 450 millions, without causing any decline in the revenues of the nation, or in trade, or in industry. It is the only kind of tax which is not destructive in an agricultural kingdom.

[2] Mirabeau explains and extends these calculations in Part One, Section Four, which deals specifically with 'the *Tableau Économique* considered relatively to the amount of taxes and tithes'. As stated in footnote on p. 129 above, he there presents a second *Tableau* in which

I have departed from the hypothesis which restricted us to a consideration of the revenue of the proprietors in abstraction from taxes and tithes, only in order to round off and follow through to the end the calculation relating to population, by implying these additions to subsistence. Save for this, I now go back to the original restrictions.

There are, then, one million proprietors, whose average expenditure is estimated at 600 livres each, and three million heads of families engaged in remunerative work or employment. That makes, through the instrumentality of the additions of which we have just spoken, 471 livres for each head of family in this class, as we shall see later from the total of the annual product, which, on the present hypothesis, yields for men's expenditure 2 milliards 13 millions,[1] from which must be deducted the personal expenditure of the proprietors. The remainder goes to the class engaged in remunerative work or employment.

The 600 millions of revenue may be divided among a smaller number of proprietors. In that case, the fewer proprietors there were, the more would the expenditure of their revenue exceed the amount which each of them would personally be able to

---

the revenue (now taken as including taxes and tithes) is 1050 livres; the annual advances of the productive class and the sterile class are 1050 and 525 livres respectively; and the total reproduction is 2705 livres. Since this second *Tableau* is the starting-point for Mirabeau's analysis of certain 'dérangements' of the economic process in the next two sections included in these extracts, it is reproduced on p. 137.

---

[1] This calculation is made in Part One, Section Six, which is not included in these extracts. Mirabeau there sets out to show that if things were ordered according to the Physiocratic prescriptions the territory of France could easily produce a 'total annual reproduction' (i.e. net revenue, plus the reproduction of the annual advances of the productive class, plus interest on these annual advances and the original advances) amounting to 2,538,334,000 livres. In order to arrive at the amount available annually for *men's* expenditure, Mirabeau deducts from this total the amount spent on the upkeep of livestock, which is assumed to be equal to one-half of the annual advances of the productive class—i.e. 525,000,000 livres. This is the origin of the figure of 2 milliards 13 millions given in the text above for men's expenditure. On the assumption that there are one million proprietors who spend 600 each, that leaves us with 1 milliard 413 millions for division among the remaining three million heads of families—i.e. with 471 livres for each, as stated in the text.

TABLEAU ŒCONOMIQUE.

OBJETS à confidérer : 1°. *trois fortes de depenſes* ; 2°. *leur ſource*, 3°. *leurs avances*, 4°. *leur diſtribution* ; 5°. *leurs effets*, 6°. *leur réproduction* ; 7°. *leurs rapports entr'elles*, 8°. *leurs rapports avec la population* , 9°. *avec l'Agriculture* , 10°. *avec l'induſtrie* , 11°. *avec le commerce* , 12°. *avec la maſſe des richeſſes d'une Nation.*

DÉPENSES PRODUCTIVES relatives à l'Agriculture, &c.	DEPENSES DU REVENU, l'Impôt & la dixme, qui ſe partagent aux dépenſes productives & aux dépenſes ſtériles.	DÉPENSES STÉRILES relatives à l'induſtrie , &c.

AVANCES ANNUELLES pour produire un revenu de 600 *l*. l'Impôt de 300 *l*. la dixme de 150 *l*. ſont 1050 *l*. 2050ᴸ produiſent net.....................1050ᴸ

REVENU annuel de

AVANCES ANNUELLES pour les Ouvrages des dépenſes ſtériles ſont   525ᴸ

PRODUCTIONS.   OUVRAGES, &c.

525ᴸ reproduiſent net..................525ᴸ.......................525ᴸ

262. 10 ſ. reproduiſent net...........262. 10 ſ..................262. 10. ſ.

131. 5. reproduiſent net...........131. 5.   131. 5.

65. 12. 6. d. reproduiſent net.......65. 12. 6. d.   65. 12. 6. d.

32. 16 3. reproduiſent net...........32. 16. 3.   32. 16. 3.

16. 8. 1. reproduiſent net...........16. 8. 1.   16. 8. 1.

8. 4. 0. reproduiſent net.........8. 4. 0.   8. 4. 0.

4. 2. 0. reproduiſent net.........4. 2. 0.   4. 2. 0.

2. 1. 0. reproduiſent net...........2. 1. 0.   1. 0.

1. 0. 6. reproduiſent net.........1. 0. 6.   1. 0. 6.

0. 10. 3. reproduiſent net...........0. 10. 3.   0. 10. 3.

0. 5. 1. reproduiſent net...........0. 5. 1.   0. 5. 1.

0. 2. 6. reproduiſent net...........0. 2. 6.   0. 2. 6.

&c.

REPRODUIT TOTAL . . . . . 1050. *liv*. de revenu. De plus les frais annuels de 1050. *liv*. & les intérêts des avances annuelles & des avances primitives du Laboureur, de 605. *liv*. que la terre reſtitue. Ainſi la reproduction eſt de 2705 *liv*. compris le revenu de 600. *liv*. qui eſt la baſe du calcul du produit total annuel de la moitié de l'emploi d'une charruë. Ainſi le produit de l'emploi entier d'une charruë en grande culture, peut être eſtimée, du fort au foible, à 5410. *liv*.

Mirabeau's second *Tableau*, in which the revenue is increased to include taxes and tithes.

consume. But then they would indulge in liberality, or gather together other men to consume with them what their revenue provided for their expenditure, so that this expenditure would turn out to be distributed in almost the same way as if there had been a greater number of proprietors limited to a smaller individual expenditure. We should regard in the same way inequalities in the gains or profits of men in the other classes, within which the advances, the interest, and the profits of entrepreneurs in agriculture, commerce, manufactures, etc., are passed on to the workmen. These things provide, by means of a mutual distribution which proceeds round by round in successive steps, gains or wages for all men who carry on remunerative occupations. Thus it comes about that the expenditure of wealth is only a distribution and transference of expenditure, which is spread out among all the other citizens in accordance with the kind of reward they receive.

PART TWO, SECTION ONE

The Tableau Économique
Considered in Connection with its Private Depredations

Excessive Luxury

Let us now study the Tableau Économique in connection with its derangements. We shall consider it in this regard from only seven points of view: (1) in connection with its private depredations, i.e. the derangements which arise from the manners of a nation and from its ignorance. The other six aspects are public depredations, namely, (2) relatively to the spoliation of the productive advances; (3) relatively to population; (4) in relation to the money stock; (5) in relation to civil administration; (6) in relation to trade; and finally (7) relatively to destructive taxes.[1]

Properly considered, derangements of manners and the

---

[1] Mirabeau's discussion of aspects (3) to (7) is not included in these extracts.

absurdities of ignorance always arise from some public error; but if it is one of my aims to investigate physical miscalculations and to rectify them at their very root, it is not another to attack moral illusions in the same way. Thus when the reader sees me use the word *luxury* here, let him not expect it to have the abundance of senses which this word suggests to the citizen heart. I speak here only of physical luxury.

In the new plate which I now present,[1] the *Tableau* has lost its equilibrium. It is a question of perceiving and explaining the causes and effects of this derangement. We have seen from the very first steps in the explanation of the *Tableau* that the distribution of the revenue of the proprietor through the instrumentality of his expenditure is what alone gives motion to the machine of circulation. We can easily see that this expenditure may go more or less to one side or the other, according as the man who engages in it goes in more or less for luxury in the way of subsistence [*luxe de subsistance*] or for luxury in the way of ornamentation [*luxe de décoration*], which can alone be properly called *luxury*.

Formerly in the *Tableau Économique* we have assumed a medium situation in which the reproductive expenditure renews the same revenue from year to year; but it is easy to estimate the changes which would take place in the annual reproduction, according as reproductive expenditure or sterile expenditure preponderated. It is easy to estimate them, I say, from the changes which would occur in the *Tableau*.

It is in this situation that we present it here. We assume that luxury in the way of ornamentation increases by one-sixth in the case of the proprietor, that is, that he pays back an additional 87 livres to the sterile expenditure side,[2] which means a transfer of 612 livres 10 sous to that column, and reduces the payment to the productive column to 437 livres 10 sous. Manners follow one another and are spread out by imitation

---

[1] See the *Tableau* reproduced on p. 140 below. It should be noted that the figure given in this *Tableau* for the annual advances of the sterile class should be 525, not 300.

[2] Actually 87 livres 10 sous. The assumption is that the proprietor, who formerly spent one-half of his revenue of 1050 livres on the products of the sterile class, now increases this expenditure by one-sixth—i.e. to a total of 612 livres 10 sous.

TABLEAU ŒCONOMIQUE.

OBJETS à considérer : *Depradations privées, Mœurs & Usages civils, Excès, le Luxe.*

DÉPENSES PRODUCTIVES relatives à l'Agriculture, &c.	DÉPENSES DU REVENU, l'Impôt & la dixme, qui se partagent aux dépenses productives & aux dépenses stériles.	DÉPENSES STÉRILES relatives à l'industrie, &c.

AVANCES ANNUELLES pour produire un revenu de 600 l. l'Impôt de 300 l. la dixme de 150 l. sont 1050 l.   REVENU annuel de   AVANCES ANNUELLES pour les Ouvrages des dépenses stériles sont,

1050ᵗ produisent net................1050ᵗ   300ᵗ

PRODUCTIONS.   OUVRAGES, &c.

437. 10. f. reproduisent net........437. 10. f. ....612. 10. f.

255. 4. 2. d. reproduisent net......255. 4. 2. d. ....255. 4. 2. d.

106. 6. 8. reproduisent net.........106. 6. 8. ....148. 17. 5.

62. 0. 7. reproduisent net..........62. 0. 7. ....62. 0. 7.

25. 17. 0. reproduisent net.........25. 17. 0. ....36. 3. 8.

15. 1. 7. reproduisent net..........15. 1. 7. ....15. 1. 7.

6. 5. 8. reproduisent net...........6. 5. 8. ....8. 15. 11.

3. 13. 3. reproduisent net..........3. 13. 3. ....3. 13. 3.

1. 10. 6. reproduisent net..........1. 10. 6. ....2. 2. 8.

0. 17. 9. reproduisent net..........0. 17. 9. ....0. 17. 9.

0. 7. 4. reproduisent net...........0. 7. 4. ....0. 10. 4.

0. 4. 3. reproduisent net...........0. 4. 3. ....0. 4. 3.

0. 1. 9. reproduisent net...........0. 1. 9. ....0. 2. 5.
&c.

REPRODUIT TOTAL...... 915. *liv.* de revenu. De plus les frais annuels de 915. *liv.* & les interêts des avances annuelles & des avances primitives du Laboureur, de 527. *liv.* que la terre restitue. Ainsi la reproduction n'est que de 2357. *liv.* au lieu de 2705. *liv.* C'est 348. *liv.* de perte, ou environ deux cinquiémes.

The *Tableau* to which Part Two, Section One of Mirabeau's explanation refers.

through all classes, since the moral concatenation is everywhere the same as the physical concatenation. This radical change of one-sixth will be the same in the case of the artisan and in that of the cultivator, whence it results that when we follow the progression of the *Tableau*, in accordance with this new state of affairs, we find at the foot that the total reproduction of revenue of 1050 livres, including taxes and tithes, is reduced from 1050 livres to 915 livres, and the returns of the husband-man of 1655 livres are reduced to 1442 livres,[1] so that the total decrease is 348 livres—i.e. a loss of about two-fifteenths.

If on the other hand an increase of the same degree took place in expenditure on the consumption or export of the pro-duce of the soil, the revenue reproduced of 1050 livres would rise to 1146 livres, and the returns of the husbandman of 1655 livres would then amount to 1806 livres, i.e. they would in-crease by 151 livres.[2] Thus the total increase would be 247 livres, or about one-tenth; and so on in progression, to the extent that cultivation and the soil were able to help bring this about.

It is this latter effect which is secured through a constant and sustained rise in primary produce; and it is in this way that blind men who are obstinately set on keeping its price low do great damage, without being aware of it, to the revenue and subsistence of the nation.

We see from this very simple demonstration that an opulent

---

[1] The new 'revenue' figure of 915 livres is obtained by summing the figures in the central column, which (on the assumption that agricul-ture 'yields 100 per cent') are identical with the figures for the mone-tary receipts of the husbandman in the left-hand column. The new 'returns of the husbandman' figure of 1442 livres is obtained by adding to the husbandman's receipts of 915 livres the sum of 527 livres for interest, the latter being approximately $\frac{915}{1050}$ of the basic figure of 605 livres given for interest in the *Tableau* on p. 137. See footnote on p. 129 above.

[1] The new 'revenue' figure of 1146 livres is obtained by summing the receipts in the right-hand column, to which the figures for the mone-tary receipts of the husbandman, and therefore for the 'revenue', would be identical if an 'increase of the same degree' took place in expenditure on the products of the productive class. The new 'returns of the husbandman' figure is obtained by adding to the husbandman's receipts of 1146 livres a figure of $\frac{1146}{1050}$ of ·605, i.e. 660 livres, for interest.

nation which indulges in excessive luxury in the way of ornamentation can very quickly be overwhelmed by its sumptuousness. We also see how essential it is to maintain opulence among the different orders of men who according to the accepted customs of society are allowed to employ their superfluity in luxury in the way of subsistence, since wealthy people of humble origin are, so to speak, forced by the prejudices of society to cultivate a taste for expenditure on studied refinement, and are unable to broaden out into luxury in the way of subsistence, which would be a burden to them and make them look ridiculous.

We can similarly understand how little versed people still were in economic matters in a country where a charge on servants and on the horses which consume corn, fodder, and the other produce of the productive class, was described as a tax on luxury.

Thus it is not true that the type of expenditure is a matter of indifference.

[*The remainder of this section, which deals mainly with the advantages to be gained from large-scale cultivation by wealthy farmers, is omitted.*]

PART TWO, SECTION TWO

The Tableau Économique
Considered Relatively to Spoliation

We have just dealt with a kind of depredation whose effects are certainly very great and which may become excessively so, depending upon the extent of the state and the territory of the nation whose manners decline in this way. But important though it may be, it is not through its physical effects that it can so quickly succeed in ruining a nation and reducing it to the level of poverty relatively to its product in which we are going to depict it. Rather, it may do this through its moral effects, in that the disorder concerned introduces and necessitates greed, which is always blind in the means it adopts to attain its ends.

TABLEAU ŒCONOMIQUE.

CE TABLEAU montre les effets rapides de la spoliation du fonds des avances ; spoliation provenante, soit de l'Impôt ; soit de toute autre cause, c'est-à-dire de tout fléau portant sur les avances de la culture. On suppose 50. liv. ôtées par an sur les avances de 1050. liv. ce qui les réduit d'abord à 1000. livres.

DÉPENSES PRODUCTIVES relatives à l'Agriculture, &c.	DÉPENSES DU REVENU, l'Impôt & la dîme, qui se partagent aux dépenses productives & aux dépenses stériles.	DÉPENSES STÉRILES relatives à l'Industrie, &c.

AVANCES ANNUELLES pour produire un revenu de 1000. liv. sont 1000. l.   REVENU annuel de   AVANCES ANNUELLES pour les Ouvrages des dépenses stériles sont,

1000ᵗᵗ produisent net..............1000ᵗᵗ   500ᵗᵗ

PRODUCTIONS.   OUVRAGES, &c.

500ᵗᵗ. reproduisent net...........500ᵗᵗ   500ᵗᵗ

250. reproduisent net............250.   250.

125. reproduisent net............125.   125.

62. 10. s. reproduisent net.........62. 10. s.   62. 10. s.

31. 5. reproduisent net............31. 5.   31. 5.

15. 12. 6. d. reproduisent net.....15. 12. 6. d.   15. 12. 6. d.

7. 16. 3. reproduisent net.........7. 16. 3.   7. 16. 3.

3. 18. 1. reproduisent net.........3. 18. 1.   3. 18. 1.

1. 19. 0. reproduisent net.........1. 19. 0.   1. 19. 0.

0. 19. 6. reproduisent net........0. 19. 6.   0. 19. 6.

0. 9. 9. reproduisent net.........0. 9. 9.   0. 9. 9.

0. 4. 10. reproduisent net........0. 4. 10.   0. 4. 10.

0. 2. 5. reproduisent net.........0. 2. 5.   0. 2. 5.

&c.

REPRODUIT TOTAL..... 1000. liv. de revenu. De plus les frais annuels de 1000. liv. & les intérêts des avances annuelles & des avances primitives du Laboureur, de 577. liv. que la terre restitue. Ainsi la reproduction est de 2577. l. au lieu de 2705. liv. & le Cultivateur a perdu 50. liv. sur le produit, 50. liv. sur les avances, & 28. liv. sur les intérêts de ses avances ; ce qui diminue la reproduction de 128. livres.

The *Tableau* to which Part Two, Section Two of Mirabeau's explanation refers.

The case of real and rapid deterioration whose effects, so startling in the calculation, are even more deplorable in actual fact, is spoliation.

We understand by this word any excessive burden whatever, whether arising from taxes or from any other affliction—any excessive burden, I say, which is borne by the fund of advances for cultivation, and which results in a loss to the fund of these advances.

To construct the *Tableau* on this hypothesis, we continue to present it here in its fully extended form—that is, including in it the taxes and tithes together with the revenue of the proprietors; but we assume that one or other of the above-mentioned misunderstandings or misfortunes takes away 50 livres per year from the annual advances of 1050 livres necessary for reproduction. This deduction reduces them to 1000 livres, and it is on this basis that we construct the *Tableau*.[1]

We see from the summary at the foot of this *Tableau* that the total reproduction is 1000 livres of revenue; in addition, the annual costs of 1000 livres, and the interest on the annual and original advances of the husbandmen, worked out according to the same progression as all the rest, amounting to 577 livres.[2] Thus the total reproduction is 2577 livres.

If we compare this product with that which the *Tableau* formerly gave us, when it was in its state of complete immunity, we shall find that the first one gave us 2705 livres, whereas this one from the first year gives us no more than 2577 livres. Thus there is a diminution of 128 livres in the reproduction. The cultivator has in fact lost 50 livres on the net product, 50 livres on the annual advances, and 28 livres on the interest on his advances, which makes a total loss of 128 livres; and the whole of this loss arises from the original spoliation of 50 livres on the fund of advances. So that we should not think that this is merely a game, let us remember that our livres are millions of livres.

Assuming that the affliction which has done us so great an injury is of such a kind as to be lasting, our progression must be continued, by giving the horse full rein. We shall find that in the second year the continued spoliation of 50 livres per annum

[1] See the *Tableau* reproduced on p. 143 above.
[2] 577 livres = (approximately) $\frac{1000}{1050}$ of ·605 livres.

will cause a loss of 455 livres, in the third 1293 livres, and in the fourth 3438 livres.[1]

It necessarily follows that this loss will be borne by the original advances, since the annual advances, amounting in their entirety to only 1050 livres, will be more than swallowed up. Thus we have a loss of 5314 livres in four years, taken out of the fund of original advances for the establishment of one plough.[2] We have said that these advances, with cultivation in a good state, may be estimated at ten thousand livres. Thus it would be true to say that in four years the plough would be cut by a half—that is, completely disabled, for the same reason that when one of the two horses pulling a carriage falls the other must come to a stop.

To get round this fatal difficulty, the cultivator adopts the disastrous method of retrenching all parts of his advances, of putting less into manure, less into livestock, and less into hands; of having oxen or ponies draw his plough, and of giving the soil fewer and less heavy dressings. But all this comes to the same thing so far as the product is concerned. Whether we are stung on the head or the heel, the pain makes itself felt just the same over the whole frame. Similarly in agriculture, whatever it may be that the farmer lacks, whether dressing, or good quality seed, etc., the loss—more or less obvious, more or less vital—is always a loss, and at harvest-time is revealed as such for the cultivator, the proprietor and the state.

If we ask why it is, then, that a whole kingdom in which agriculture is going this way does not find itself lying completely waste at the end of eight years, the answer is that the spoliation of which we are speaking brings about an arbitrary and successive disturbance of distribution which does not ruin all the farmers at the same time. It is like a host of worms eating away inch by inch the roots of the plants in a garden, and in time finishing up by destroying the garden itself. I could also reply that there have never been any more barbarous spoliators—at any rate among those who have used force openly—than the

---

[1] The basis of Mirabeau's calculations here is not at all clear, but the sums work out reasonably well if one assumes that in each year after the first the cultivator in effect employs annual advances of 1000 livres *minus* the previous year's 'loss'.

[2] See footnote 1 on p. 127 above.

Huns of olden times. After they had been repelled, and their
refuge in Pannonia was stormed, treasures were found accumulated behind their gates; and although these treasures were
a very small matter alongside the wealth which the Huns had
destroyed throughout Europe, they were nevertheless immense
by comparison with the little which remained elsewhere. Thus
all spoliation implies that there is a robbers' lair in which the
debris which has been carried off in the ravages is accumulated.
Assuming that these ravages had been of a kind to lend the
spoliation a civil character, the enjoyment of the fruits resulting
from it would be allowable and customary in the places of
residence of the spoliators; and if this residence were at the
centre of the ravaged state, the consumption and expenditure
of every kind of its inhabitants would necessarily support the
revival of its outskirts, and maintain large-scale cultivation
there for some time longer.

It might even happen, if these outskirts were employed in
the production of goods of primary necessity, that the nicety of
taste of the inhabitants, and the superfluity they possessed,
would lead them to try to obtain products of secondary necessity from distant regions. The sun does not get out of order as
the equation of products does; it may produce oils in one of the
subjugated countries and fine wines in another, and scatter
partridges and garden buntings elsewhere; and the pursuit of
all these things would send out small offshoots of revival to the
ravaged countries.

These same offshoots, whether issuing from the capital or
from other storehouses of false subsistence, would maintain
the capacity of some parts of the territory—in the midst of a large
amount of fallow or waste land—to yield twenty per cent of the
advances of cultivation, while one would still find parts under
large-scale cultivation in districts allotted to the direct consumption of the principal place of residence.

[*The last three paragraphs of this section, which deal mainly
with the encouragement which it is necessary to give to
agriculture when the state is in an ' exhausted condition', are
omitted.*]

Sir James Steuart

FIVE EXTRACTS FROM
AN INQUIRY INTO THE PRINCIPLES
OF POLITICAL OECONOMY
(1767)

Source: The first extract reprinted here—from Book I, Chapter V—consists only of the last few paragraphs of the chapter concerned. All the other chapters, however, are reprinted in their entirety. The text used is that of the first (1767) edition, the detailed page references being respectively pp. 30–1, 31–6, 181–3, 216–25, and 225–32, all of Vol. I. Steuart's footnotes are keyed in by asterisks, and the present editor's by numerical indicators.

Sir James Steuart (1713–80) threw in his lot with Prince Charles in 1745, and was sent to France in that year to negotiate for assistance from the French. After Culloden he remained in France, and was unable to return home from exile until 1763. His massive work *An Inquiry into the Principles of Political Oeconomy*, which he began to write while he was in France, was published in 1767. He died four years after the appearance of the *Wealth of Nations*, in which his *Inquiry* was never once referred to.

It is hardly surprising that Smith should have had little sympathy for Steuart's work, which was tinged in places with 'Mercantilist' notions, which underestimated the capacity of the economic system to readjust itself when the 'balance' between demand and supply was disturbed, and in which the role allotted to the 'statesman' in economic affairs was much more active than that which Smith was prepared to allot to him. In addition to this, the model of society which Steuart postulated was far from visualizing the capitalists as an independent 'constituent order'. It was largely because of all this, no doubt, that Smith failed to show any appreciation of certain important positive features of Steuart's work—the fact that his 'Mercantilism' was really very enlightened, for example, and that his 'statesman' was constantly enjoined to operate through rather than in opposition to 'the principle of self-interest'.[1] Nor was Steuart's theory of value without certain very positive merits: his treatment of the 'balance' of supply and demand was quite advanced for its time, and his effort to solve the problem of the place of profit in the equilibrium price was at any rate more successful than those of most of his predecessors.

The first of our extracts—a short passage from the end of Book I, Chapter V (below, pp. 151–2)—summarizes Steuart's account of the basic division of society into 'farmers' and 'free

[1] See in particular pp. 162–5 of Vol. I of Steuart's *Inquiry* (1st edn., 1767).

hands',[1] which is very similar to Hume's. It is more fully worked out than Hume's, however, and is put forward in the context of an interesting theory of the early development of society which bears a distinct family resemblance to the 'sociological' theories elaborated by Turgot, the Physiocrats and the members of the Scottish Historical School.[2]

The second extract (below, pp. 152–6) illustrates the emphasis which Steuart placed throughout his book on the influence of changing patterns of demand on the development of the economy; and the third (pp. 157–8) contains his account of the basic constituents of the equilibrium prices of commodities. Here it is his distinction between the 'real value' of a commodity—equal, roughly, to producers' costs excluding profit— and what he calls the 'profit upon alienation' (p. 157)[3] which is important. The price of the commodity, he argues, cannot be *lower* than the 'real value', and the extent to which it is in fact *higher* represents the manufacturer's profit (p. 158). The latter, says Steuart, 'will ever be in proportion to demand, and there- fore will fluctuate according to circumstances'—a viewpoint which leaves profit essentially indeterminate.

The fourth extract (below, pp. 159–66), entitled 'Of the Balance of Work and Demand', contains Steuart's elaborate and striking account of the interaction of supply and demand in a market economy, and in particular of the ways in which the 'balance' between the two may be 'overturned'. It is apparent from this section of his book that Steuart's concept of profit is very different from Smith's: 'profit' for Steuart evidently meant any kind of net gain (over and above 'real value') which accrued to anyone engaged in production or trade, whether as an employer, a wage-earner, or a worker on his own account. It is only very rarely in the *Inquiry* that Steuart makes a dis-

[1] In Book I, Chapter ix of the *Inquiry* the 'free hands' who 'live upon the surplus of the farmers' are subdivided into 'those to whom this surplus directly belongs, or who, with a revenue in money already acquired, can purchase it', and 'those who purchase it with their daily labour or personal service' (*Inquiry*, Vol. I, p. 48).

[2] The chapters in which Steuart elaborates this theory of the early development of society are not included in our extracts.

[3] The term 'profit upon alienation', with its implication that profit is generated in exchange rather than in production, is itself very significant.

tinction between capitalists and wage-earners, and there is scarcely any recognition of the importance of the role of capital in production. But there is at least an appreciation of the fact that competition will reduce profits to a 'proper standard' or a 'reasonable' level,[1] and in his theory of the 'consolidation' of profits—i.e., in effect, their incorporation over time into the supply prices of commodities (pp. 163–5)—Steuart came much closer to the Classical theory than he has usually been given credit for doing. In Smith's eyes, however, this advance must have appeared to be vastly outweighed by Steuart's obvious underestimation of the capacity of the system to readjust itself, without the active aid of the 'statesman', when the 'balance' was 'overturned'.

The final extract (below, pp. 166–72), in which Steuart tries to graft a long-period analysis on to the short-period analysis of the previous chapter, is noteworthy for its adumbration of the notion of diminishing returns in agriculture, and has a distinctly 'Ricardian' flavour about it. Once again, however, Smith could hardly have been expected to approve of it, partly because of its continued emphasis on the economic role of the 'statesman', and partly because of its underlying idea that a 'natural stop' must eventually be put to 'augmentations of every kind' (p. 167).

AN INQUIRY INTO THE PRINCIPLES OF POLITICAL OECONOMY

From Book I, Chapter V[2]

... Let me now put an end to this chapter, by drawing some conclusions from what has been laid down, in order to enlarge our ideas, and to enable us to extend our plan.

I. One consequence of a fruitful soil, possessed by a free

---

[1] *Inquiry*, Vol. I, pp. 490 and 199.
[2] The title of this chapter is: 'In what Manner, and according to what Principles, and *political Causes*, does Agriculture augment Population?'

people, given to agriculture, and inclined to industry, will be the production of a superfluous quantity of food, over and above what is necessary to feed the farmers. Inhabitants will multiply; and according to their increase, a certain number of the whole, proportional to such superfluity of nourishment produced, will apply themselves to industry and to the supplying of other wants.

II. From this operation produced by industry, we find the people distributed into two classes. The first is that of the farmers who produce the subsistence, and who are necessarily employed in this branch of business; the other I shall call *free hands;* because their occupation being to procure themselves subsistence out of the superfluity of the farmers, and by a labour adapted to the wants of the society, may vary according to these wants, and these again according to the spirit of the times.

III. If in the country we are treating of, both money and the luxurious arts are supposed unknown, then the superfluity of the farmers will be in proportion to the number of those whose labour will be found sufficient to provide for all the other necessities of the inhabitants; and so soon as this is accomplished, the consumption and produce becoming equally balanced, the inhabitants will increase no more, or at least very precariously, unless their wants be multiplied.

BOOK I, CHAPTER VI

How the Wants of Mankind promote their Multiplication.

If the country we were treating of in the former chapter be supposed of a considerable extent and fruitfulness, and if the inhabitants have a turn for industry; in a short time, *luxury* and the use of *money* (or of something participating of the nature of money) will infallibly be introduced.

By LUXURY, I understand *the consumption of any thing produced by the labour or ingenuity of man, which flatters our senses or taste of living, and which is neither necessary for our being well*

*fed, well clothed, well defended against the injuries of the weather,
nor for securing us against every thing which can hurt us.**

By MONEY, I understand *any commodity, which purely in
itself is of no material use to man for the purposes above-mentioned,
but which acquires such an estimation from his opinion of it, as to
become the universal measure of what is called value, and an
adequate equivalent for any thing alienable.*

Here a new scene opens. This money must be found in the
hands of some of the inhabitants; naturally, of such as have had
the wit to invent it, and the address to make their countrymen
fond of it, by representing it as an equivalent value for food
and necessaries; that is to say, the means of procuring, without
work or toil, not only the labour of others, but food itself.

Here then is produced a new object of want. Every person
becomes fond of having money; but how to get it is the question. The proprietors will not give it for nothing, and by our
former supposition every one within the society was understood
to be abundantly supplied with food and necessaries; the
farmers, from their labouring the ground; the free hands, by
the return of their own ingenuity, in furnishing necessaries.
The proprietors therefore of this money have all their wants

* As my subject is different from that of morals, I have no occasion
to consider the term luxury in any other than a political sense, to wit,
as a principle which produces employment, and gives bread to those
who supply the demands of the rich. For this reason I have chosen the
above definition of it, which conveys no idea, either of abuse,
sensuality, or excess; nor do I, at present, even consider the hurtful
consequences of it as to foreign trade. Principles here are treated of
with regard to mankind in general, and the effects of luxury are only
considered relatively to multiplication and agriculture. Our reasoning
will take a different turn, when we come to examine the separate
interest of nations, and the principles of trade.

I beg therefore, that at present my reasoning be carried no further
(from inductions and suppositions) than my intention is that it should
be. I am no patron, cither of vice, profusion, or the dissipation of private fortunes; although *I may now and then reason very cooly upon
the political consequences of such diseases in a state, when I only consider
the influence they have as to feeding and multiplying a people.* My subject
is too extensive of itself to admit of being confounded with the doctrine
either of morals, or of government, however closely these may appear
connected with it; and did I not begin by simplifying ideas as much as
possible, and by banishing combinations, I should quickly lose my
way, and involve myself in perplexities inextricable.

supplied, and still are possessors of this new kind of riches, which we now suppose to be coveted by all.

The natural consequence here will be, that those who have the money will cease to labour, and yet will consume; and they will not consume for nothing, for they will pay with money.

Here then is a number of inhabitants, who live and consume the produce of the earth without labouring: food will soon become scarce; demand for it will rise, and that will be paid with money; this is the best equivalent of all; many will run to the plough; the superfluity of the farmers will augment; the rich will call for superfluities; the free hands will supply them, and demand food in their turn. These will not be found a burden on the husbandmen, as formerly; the rich, who hired of them their labour or service, must pay them with money, and this money in their hands will serve as an equivalent for the superfluity of nourishment produced by additional agriculture.

When once this imaginary wealth, money, becomes well introduced into a country, luxury will very naturally follow; and when money becomes the object of our wants, mankind become industrious, in turning their labour towards every object which may engage the rich to part with it; and thus the inhabitants of any country may increase in numbers, until the ground refuses farther nourishment. The consequences of this will make the subject of another chapter.[1]

Before we proceed, something must be said, in order to restrain these general assertions a little.

We have supposed a very rapid progress of industry, and a very sudden augmentation of inhabitants, from the introduction of money. But it must be observed, that many circumstances have concurred with the money, to produce this effect.

We have supposed a country capable of improvement, a laborious people, a taste of refinement and luxury in the rich, an ambition to become so, and an application to labour and ingenuity in the lower classes of men. According to the greater or less degree of force, or concurrence of these and like circumstances, will the country in question become more or less cultivated, and consequently peopled.

[1] They make the main subject of Book I, Chapter xviii (not included in these extracts), which is entitled: 'Of the Causes and Consequences of a Country's being fully peopled'.

If the soil be vastly rich, situated in a warm climate, and naturally watered, the productions of the earth will be almost spontaneous: this will make the inhabitants lazy. Laziness is the greatest of all obstacles to labour and industry. Manufactures will never flourish here. The rich, with all their money, will not become luxurious with delicacy and refinement; for I do not mean by luxury the gratification of the animal appetites, nor the abuse of riches, but *an elegance of taste and in living, which has for its object the labour and ingenuity of man;* and as the ingenuity of workmen begets a taste in the rich, so the allurement of riches kindles an ambition, and encourages an application to works of ingenuity in the poor.

Riches therefore will here be adored as a god, but not made subservient to the uses of man; and it is only by the means of swift circulation from hand to hand, (as shall be observed in its proper place) that they become productive of the effects mentioned above.*

When money does not circulate, it is the same thing as if it did not exist; and as the treasures found in countries where the inhabitants are lazy do not circulate, they are rather ornamental than useful.

It is not therefore in the most fruitful countries of the world, nor in those which are the best calculated for nourishing great multitudes, that we find the most inhabitants. It is in climates less favoured by nature, and where the soil only produces to those who labour, and in proportion to the industry of every one, where we may expect to find great multitudes; and even these will be found greater or less, in proportion as the turn of the inhabitants is directed to ingenuity and industry.

In such countries where these are made to flourish, the free hands (of whom we have spoken above) will be employed in useful manufactures, which, being refined upon by the

* Every transition of money from hand to hand, for a valuable consideration, implies some service done, something wrought by man, or performed by his ingenuity, or some consumption of something produced by his labour. The quicker therefore the circulation of money is in any country, the more strongly it may be inferred, that the inhabitants are laborious; and *vice versa:* but of this more hereafter.[1]

[1] 'Circulation' is dealt with mainly in Book II, Chapters xxvii and xxviii, neither of which is included in these extracts.

ingenious, will determine what is called the standard of taste; this taste will increase consumption, which again will multiply workmen, and these will encourage the production of food for their nourishment.

Let it therefore never be said, that there are too many manufacturers employed in a country; it is the same as if it were said, there are too few idle persons, too few beggars, and too many husbandmen.

We have more than once endeavoured to shew, that these manufacturers never can be fed but out of the superfluity of nourishment produced by the farmers. It is a contradiction, I think, to say, that those who are fed upon the surplus of those who cultivate the soil are necessary for producing a sufficiency to themselves. For if even this surplus were to diminish, the manufacturers,[1] not the labourers, would be the first to be extinguished for want of nourishment.

The importance of the distributive proportion of mankind into labourers and free hands appears so great, and has so intimate a connection with this subject, that it engages me to seek for an illustration of the principles I have been laying down, in an example drawn from facts, as it is found to stand in one of the greatest and most flourishing nations in Europe.[2] But before I proceed farther in this part of my subject, I must examine the consequences of slavery with regard to the subject we are now upon. Relations here are so many and so various, that it is necessary to have sometimes recourse to transitions, of which I give notice to my reader, that he may not lose the connection.[3]

[1] The original has 'manufactures', which is clearly an error.
[2] The 'illustration' is given in Book I, Chapter viii, which is not included in these extracts.
[3] 'The Effects of Slavery upon the Multiplication and Employment of Mankind' are discussed in Book I, Chapter vii, which is not included in these extracts.

BOOK II, CHAPTER IV

How the Prices of Goods are determined by Trade.

In the price of goods, I consider two things as really existing, and quite different from one another; to wit, the real value of the commodity, and the profit upon alienation. The intention of this chapter is to establish this distinction, and to shew how the operation of trade severally influences the standard of the one and the other; that is to say, how trade has the effect of rendering fixt and determined, two things which would otherwise be quite vague and uncertain.

I. The first thing to be known of any manufacture when it comes to be sold, is, how much of it a person can perform in a day, a week, a month, according to the nature of the work, which may require more or less time to bring it to perfection. In making such estimates, regard is to be had only to what, upon an average, a workman of the country in general may perform, without supposing him the best or the worst of his profession; or having any peculiar advantage or disadvantage as to the place where he works.

Hence the reason why some people thrive by their industry, and others not; why some manufactures flourish in one place and not in another.

II. The second thing to be known, is the value of the workman's subsistence and necessary expence, both for supplying his personal wants, and providing the instruments belonging to his profession, which must be taken upon an average as above; except when the nature of the work requires the presence of the workman in the place of consumption: for although some trades, and almost every manufacture, may be carried on in places at a distance, and therefore may fall under one general regulation as to prices, yet others there are which, by their nature, require the presence of the workman in the place of consumption; and in that case the prices must be regulated by circumstances relative to every particular place.

III. The third and last thing to be known, is the value of the materials, that is the first matter employed by the workman; and if the object of his industry be the manufacture of another, the same process of inquiry must be gone through with regard to the first, as with regard to the second: and thus the most complex manufactures may be at last reduced to the greatest simplicity. I have been more particular in this analysis of manufactures than was absolutely necessary in this place, that I might afterwards with the greater ease point out the methods of diminishing the prices of them.

These three articles being known, the price of manufacture is determined. It cannot be lower than the amount of all the three, that is, than the real value; whatever it is higher, is the manufacturer's profit. This will ever be in proportion to demand, and therefore will fluctuate according to circumstances.

Hence appears the necessity of a great demand, in order to promote flourishing manufactures.

By the extensive dealings of merchants, and their constant application to the study of the balance of work and demand, all the above circumstances are known to them, and are made known to the industrious, who regulate their living and expence according to their certain profit. I call it certain, because under these circumstances they seldom overvalue their work, and by not overvaluing it, they are sure of a sale: a proof of this may be had from daily experience.

Employ a workman in a country where there is little trade or industry, he proportions his price always to the urgency of your want, or your capacity to pay; but seldom to his own labour. Employ another in a country of trade, he will not impose upon you, unless perhaps you be a stranger, which supposes your being ignorant of the value; but employ the same workman in a work not usual in the country, consequently not demanded, consequently not regulated as to the value, he will proportion his price as in the first supposition.

We may therefore conclude from what has been said, that in a country where trade is established, manufactures must flourish, from the ready sale, the regulated price of work, and certain profit resulting from industry. Let us next inquire into the consequences of such a situation.[1]

---

[1] Chapters v and vi, in which Steuart proceeds to do this, are not included in these extracts.

BOOK II, CHAPTER X

Of the Balance of Work and Demand.

It is quite impossible to go methodically through the subject of political oeconomy, without being led into anticipations. We have frequently mentioned this balance of work and demand, and shewed how important a matter it is for a statesman to attend to it. The thing, therefore, in general is well understood; and all that remains to be done, is to render our ideas more determined concerning it, and more adequate, if possible, to the principles we have been laying down.

We have treated fully of demand, and likewise of competition.[1] We have observed how different circumstances influence these terms,[2] so as to make them represent ideas entirely different; and we have said that double competition supports the balance we are now to speak of, and that simple[3] competition overturns it.[4]

The word demand in this chapter is taken in the most simple acceptation; and when we say that the balance between work and demand is to be sustained in equilibrio, as far as possible, we mean that the quantity supplied should be in proportion to the quantity *demanded*, that is, *wanted*. While the balance stands justly poised, prices are found in the adequate proportion of the real expence of making the goods, with a small addition for profit to the manufacturer and merchant.

I have, in the fourth chapter,[5] observed how necessary a thing it is to distinguish the two constituent parts of every price; the value, and the profit. Let the number of persons be ever so great, who, upon the sale of a piece of goods, share in the profits;

[1] In Book II, the main treatment of demand occurs in Chapter ii and of competition in Chapter vii. Neither of the chapters concerned is included in these extracts.

[2] The original has 'turns', which is clearly an error.

[3] The original has 'single', but 'simple' was clearly intended.

[4] 'When *competition* is much stronger on one side of the contract than on the other, I call it *simple*. . . . *Double competition* is, when, in a certain degree, it takes place on both sides of the contract at once, or vibrates alternately from one to the other.' (Book II, Chapter vii.)

[5] Reprinted above, pp. 157–8.

it is still essential, in such enquiries as these, to suppose them distinctly separate from the real value of the commodity; and the best way possible to discover exactly the proportion between the one and the other, is by a scrupulous watchfulness over the balance we are now treating of, as we shall presently see.

The value and profits, combined in the price of a manufacture produced by one man, are easily distinguished, by means of the analysis we have laid down in the fourth chapter. As long as any market is *fully* supplied with this sort of work, and *no more;* those who are employed in it live by their trade, and gain no unreasonable profit: because there is then no violent competition upon one side only, neither between the workmen, nor between those who buy from them, and the balance gently vibrates under the influence of a double competition. This is the representation of a perfect balance.

This balance is overturned in four different ways.

Either the demand diminishes, and the work remains the same:

Or the work diminishes, and the demand remains:

Or the demand increases, and the work remains:

Or the work increases, and the demand remains.

Now each of these four combinations may, or may not, produce a competition upon one side of the contract only. This must be explained.

If demand diminishes, and work remains the same, which is the first case, either those who furnish the work will enter into competition, in which case they will hurt each other, and prices will fall below the reasonable standard of the even balance; or they will not enter into competition, and then prices continuing as formerly, the whole demand will be supplied, and the remainder of the work will lie upon hand.

This is a symptom of decaying trade.

Let us now, on the other hand, suppose demand to increase, and work to remain as before.

This example points out no diminution on either side, as was the case before, but an augmentation upon one; and is either a symptom of growing luxury at home, or of an increase in foreign trade.

Here the same alternation of circumstances occurs. The demanders will either enter into competition and raise the price

of work, or they will enter into no competition; but being determined not to exceed the ordinary standard of the perfect
balance, will defer making their provision till another time, or
supply themselves in another market; that is to say, the new
demand will cease as soon as it is made, for want of a supply.

Whenever, therefore, this perfect balance of work and demand is overturned by the force of a simple competition, or by
one of the scales preponderating, one of two things must
happen; either a part of the demand is not answered, or a part
of the goods is not sold.

These are the immediate effects of the overturning of the
balance.

Let me next point out the object of the statesman's care,
relatively to such effects, and shew the consequences of their
being neglected.

We may now simplify our ideas, and instead of the former
combinations, make use of other expressions which may
convey them.

Let us therefore say, that the *fall* or *rise* upon either side of
the balance, is *positive*, or *relative*. *Positive*, when the side we
talk of really augments beyond, or diminishes below the usual
standard. *Relative*, when there is no alteration upon the side
we speak of, and that the subversion of the balance is owing to
an alteration on the other side. As for example:

Instead of saying demand diminishes, and work remains the
same, let us say, demand diminishes *positively*, or work increases *relatively;* according as the subject may lead us to speak
either of the one or of the other. This being premised,

If the scale of work shall preponderate *positively*, it should be
inquired, whether the quantity furnished has really swelled, in
all respects, beyond the proportion of the consumption, (in
which case the statesman should diminish the number of hands,
by throwing a part of them into a new channel) or whether the
imprudence of the workmen has only made them produce their
work unseasonably; in which case, proper information, and even
assistance should be given them, to prevent merchants from
taking the advantage of their want of experience: but these last
precautions are necessary only in the infancy of industry.

If a statesman should be negligent on this occasion; if he
should allow natural consequences to follow upon one another,

just as circumstances shall determine; then it may happen, that workmen will keep upon hand that part of their goods which exceeds the demand, until necessity forces them to enter into competition with one another, and sell for what they can get. Now this competition is hurtful, because it is all on one side, and because we have supposed the preponderating of the scale of work to be an overturning of a perfect balance, which can by no means be set right, consistently with a scheme of thriving, but by the scale of demand becoming heavier, and re-establishing a double competition. Were this to happen before the workmen come to sell in competition, then the balance would again be even, after what I call *a short vibration*, which is no *subversion;* but when the scale of work remains too long in the same position, and occasions a strong, hurtful, and lasting competition, upon one side only, then, I say, the balance is *overturned;* because this diminishes the reasonable profits, or perhaps, indeed, obliges the workmen to sell below prime cost. The effect of this is, that the workmen fall into distress, and that industry suffers a discouragement; and this effect is certain.

But it may be asked, Whether, by this fall of prices, demand will not be increased? That is to say, will not the whole of the goods be sold off?

I answer, That this may, or may not, be the effect of the fall, according to circumstances: it is a contingent consequence of the simple, but not the effect of the double competition: the distress of the workmen is a certain and unavoidable consequence of the first.

But supposing this contingent consequence to happen, will it not set the balance even, by increasing the demand? I answer, the balance is then made even by a violent shock given to industry, but it is not set even from any principle which can support it, or make it flourish. Here is the criterion of a perfect balance: *A positive moderate profit must balance a positive moderate profit; the balance must vibrate, and no loss must be found on either side.* In the example before us, the balance stands even, it is true; the work and the demand are equally poised as to quantity; but it is a *relative profit*, which hangs in the scale, opposite to a *relative loss*. I wish this may be well understood; farther illustrations will make it clear.

Next, let me suppose the scale of *demand* to preponderate

positively. In this case, the statesman should be still more upon his guard, to provide a proportional supply; because the danger here may at first put on a shew of profit, and deceive him.

The consequences of this subversion of the balance are either,

1st, That a competition will take place among the demanders only, which will raise profits. Now if, after a short vibration, the supply comes to be increased by the statesman's care, no harm will ensue; competition will change sides, and profits will come down again to the perfect standard. But if the scale of demand remains preponderating, and so keeps profits high, the consequence will be, that, in a little time, not only the immediate seller of the goods, but also every one who has contributed to the manufacture, will insist upon sharing these new profits. Now the evil is not, that every one should share, or that the profits should swell, as long as they are supported by demand, and as long as they can truly be considered as precarious; but the mischief is, that, in consequence of this wide repartition, and by such profits subsisting for a long time, they insensibly become *consolidated*, or, as it were, transformed into the intrinsic value of the goods. This, I say, is brought about by time; because the habitual extraordinary gains of every one employed induce the more luxurious among them to change their way of life insensibly, and fall into the habit of making greater consumptions, and engage the more slothful to remain idle, till they are exhausted. When therefore it happens, that large profits have been made for a considerable time, and that they have had the effect of forming a taste for a more expensive way of living among the industrious, it will not be the cessation of the demand, nor the swelling of the supply, which will engage them to part with their gains. Nothing will operate this effect but sharp necessity; and the bringing down of their profits, and the throwing the workmen into distress, are then simultaneous; which proves the truth of what I have said, that these profits become, by long habit, virtually *consolidated* with the real value of the merchandize. These are the consequences of a neglected simple competition, which raises the profits upon industry, and keeps the balance overturned for a considerable time.

2dly, Let me examine the consequences of this overturn in the actual preponderancy of demand, when it does not occasion a competition among the demanders, and consequently, when it does not increase the profits upon industry.

This case can only happen, when the commodity is not a matter of great necessity, or even of great use; since the desire of procuring it is not sufficient to engage the buyers to raise their price; unless, indeed, this difference should proceed from the ease of providing the same, in other markets, as cheap as formerly. This last is a dangerous circumstance, and loudly calls for the attention of the statesman. He must prevent, by all possible means, the desertion of the market, by a speedy supply for all the demand, and must even perhaps give encouragements to manufacturers, to enable them to diminish the prices fixed by the regular standard. This is the situation of a nation which is in the way of losing branches of her foreign trade; of which afterwards.

Whatever therefore be the consequence of the actual preponderancy of the scale of demand; that is, whether it tend to raise profits, or to discredit the market; the statesman's care should be directed immediately towards making the balance come even of itself, without any shock, and that as soon as possible, by increasing the supply. For if it be allowed to stand long in this overturned state, natural consequences will operate a forced restitution; that is, the rise in the price, or the call of a foreign market, will effectually cut off a proportional part of the demand, and leave the balance in an equilibrium, disadvantageous to trade and industry.

In the former case, the manufacturers were forced to starve, by an unnatural restitution, when the relative profit and loss of individuals balanced one another. Here the manufacturers are inriched for a little time, by a rise of profits, relative to the loss the nation sustains, by not supplying the whole demand. This results from the competition of their customers; but so soon as these profits become *consolidated* with the intrinsic value, they will cease to have the advantage of profits, and, becoming in a manner necessary to the existence of the goods, will cease to be considered as advantageous. These forced restitutions then, brought about, as we have said, by selling goods below their value, by cutting off a part of the demand, or by sending it to another market, resembles the operation of a carrier, who sets his ass's burden even, by laying a stone upon the lightest end of it. He however loses none of his merchandize; but the absurdity of the statesman is still greater, for he appears willingly to open the heavy end of the load, and to throw part of his merchandize into the high-way.

I hope, by this time, I have sufficiently shewn the difference in effect between the *simple* and the *double* competition; between the *vibrations* of this balance of work and demand, and the *overturning* of it. When it vibrates in moderation, and by short alternate risings and sinkings, then industry and trade go on prosperously, and are in harmony with each other; because both parties gain. The industrious man is recompenced in proportion to his ingenuity; the intrinsic value of goods does not vary, nor deceive the merchant; profits on both sides fluctuate according to demand, but never get time to consolidate with, and swell the real value, and never altogether disappear, and starve the workman.

This happy state cannot be supported but by the care of the statesman; and when he is found negligent in the discharge of this part of his duty, the consequence is, that either the spirit of industry, which, it is supposed, has cost him much pains to cultivate, is extinguished, or the produce of it rises to so high a value, as to be out of the reach of a multitude of purchasers.

The progress towards the one or the other of these extremes is easily perceived, by attending to the successive overturnings of the balance. When these are often repeated on the same side, and the balance set right, by a succession of forced restitutions only, the same scale preponderating a-new, then is the last period soon accomplished. When, on the contrary, the overturnings are alternate, sometimes the scale of demand overturning the balance, sometimes the scale of work, the last period is more distant. Trade and industry subsist longer, but they remain in a state of perpetual convulsion. On the other hand, when the balance gently vibrates, then work and demand, that is, trade and industry, like agriculture and population, prove mutually assisting to each other, in promoting their reciprocal augmentation.

In order therefore to preserve a trading state from decline, the greatest care must be taken, to support a perfect balance between the hands employed in work and the demand for their labour. That is to say, according to former definitions, to prevent demand from ever standing long at an immoderate height, by providing at all times a supply, sufficient to answer the greatest that ever can be made: or, in other words, still, in order to accustom my readers to certain expressions, to encourage the *great*, and to discourage the *high* demand. In this case, competition will never be found too strong on either side of the contract, and profits will be moderate, but sure, on both.

If, on the contrary, there be found too many hands for the demand, work will fall too low for workmen to be able to live; or, if there be too few, work will rise, and manufactures will not be exported.

For want of this just balance, no trading state has ever been of long duration, after arriving at a certain height of prosperity. We perceive in history the rise, progress, grandeur, and decline of Sydon, Tyre, Carthage, Alexandria, and Venice, not to come nearer home. While these states were on the growing hand, they were powerful; when once they came to their height, they immediately found themselves labouring under their own greatness. The reason of this appears from what has been said.

While there is a demand for the trade of any country, inhabitants are always on the increasing hand. This is evident from what has been so often repeated in the first book, and confirmed by thousands of examples. There never was any branch of trade established in any kingdom, province, city, or even village; but such kingdom, province, &c. increased in inhabitants. While this gradual increase of people is in proportion to the growing demand for hands, the balance between work and demand is exactly kept up: but as all augmentations must at last come to a stop, when this happens, inconveniencies must ensue, greater or less, according to the negligence of the statesman, and the violence or suddenness of the revolution.

BOOK II, CHAPTER XI

Why in Time this Balance is destroyed.

Now let us examine what may be the reason why, in a trading and industrious nation, time necessarily destroys the perfect balance between work and demand.

We have already pointed out one general cause, to wit, the natural stop which must at last be put to augmentations of every kind.

Let us now apply this to circumstances, in order to discover in what manner natural causes operate this stop, either by preventing the increase of work, on one side of the balance, or the increase of demand, on the other. When once we discover how the stop is put to augmentations, we may safely conclude, that the continuation of the same, or similar causes, will soon produce a diminution, and operate a decline.

We have traced the progress of industry, and shewn how it goes hand in hand with the augmentation of subsistence, which is the principal allurement to labour.[1] Now the augmentation of food is relative to the soil, and as long as this can be brought to produce, at an expence proportioned to the value of the returns, agriculture, without any doubt, will go forward in every country of industry. But so soon as the progress of agriculture demands an additional expence, which the natural return, at the stated prices of subsistence, will not defray, agriculture comes to a stop, and so would numbers, did not the consequences of industry push them forward, in spite of small difficulties. The industrious then, I say, continue to multiply, and the consequence is, that food becomes scarce, and that the inhabitants enter into competition for it.

This is no contingent consequence, it is an infallible one; because food is an article of the first necessity, and here the provision is supposed to fall short of the demand. This raises the profits of those who have food ready to sell; and as the balance upon this article must remain overturned for some time, without the interposition of the statesman, these profits will be consolidated with the price, and give encouragement to a more expensive improvement of the soil. I shall here interrupt the examination of the consequences of this revolution as to agriculture, until I have examined the effects which the rise of the price of food produces on industry, and on the demand for it.

This augmentation on the value of subsistence must necessarily raise the price of all work, because we are here speaking of an industrious people fully employed, and because sub-

[1] See, for example, the passages reprinted above, pp. 151–2.

sistence is one of the three articles which compose the intrinsic value of their work, as has been said.[1]

The rise therefore, upon the price of work, not being any augmentation of that part of the price which we call profits, as happens to be the case when a rise in demand has produced a competition among the buyers, cannot be brought down but by increasing the supply of subsistence; and were a statesman to mistake the real cause of the rise, and apply the remedy of increasing the quantity of work, in order to bring down the market, instead of augmenting the subsistence, he would occasion a great disorder; he would introduce the hurtful simple competition between people who labour for moderate profits, mentioned in the last chapter, and would throw such a discouragement upon their industry, as would quickly extinguish it altogether.

On the other hand, did he imprudently augment the subsistence, by large importations, he would put an end to the expensive improvement of the soil, and this whole enterprize would fall to nothing. Here then is a dilemma, out of which he can extricate himself by a right application of public money, only.

Such a necessary rise in the price of labour may either affect foreign exportation, or it may not, according to circumstances. If it does, the price of subsistence, at any rate, must be brought down at least to those who supply the foreign demand; if it does not affect foreign exportation, matters may be allowed to go on; but still the remedy must be ready at hand, to be applied the moment it becomes expedient.

There is one necessary augmentation upon the prices of industry, brought about by a very natural cause, viz. the increase of population, which may imply a more expensive improvement of the soil; that is, an extension of agriculture. This augmentation may very probably put a stop to the augmentation of demand for many branches of manufactures, consequently may stop the progress of industry; and if the same causes continue to operate in a greater degree, it may also cut off a part of the former demand, may discredit the market, open a door to foreign consumption, and produce the inconvenien-

[1] See the passage reprinted on p. 157 above.

cies of poverty and distress, in proportion to the degree of negligence in the statesman.

I shall now give another example, of a very natural augmentation upon the intrinsic value of work, which does not proceed from the increase of population, but from the progress of industry itself; which implies no internal vice in a state, but which is the necessary consequence of the reformation of a very great one. This augmentation must be felt less or more in every country, in proportion as industry becomes extended.

We have said, that the introduction of manufactures naturally tends to purge the lands of superfluous mouths: now this is a very slow and gradual operation. A consequence of it was said to be (Book I. Chap. xx)[1] an augmentation of the price of labour, because those who have been purged off, must begin to gain their whole subsistence at the expence of those who employ them.

If therefore, in the infancy of industry, any branch of it shall find itself assisted in a particular province, by the cheap labour of those mouths superfluously fed by the land, examples of which are very frequent, this advantage must diminish, in proportion as the cause of it ceases; that is, in proportion as industry is extended, and as the superfluous mouths are of consequence purged off.

This circumstance is of the last importance to be attended to by a statesman. Perhaps it was entirely owing to it, that industry was enabled to set up its head in this corner. How many examples could I give, of this assistance given to manufactures in different provinces, where I have found the value of a day's work, of spinning, for example, not equal to half the nourishment of the person. This is a great encouragement to the making of cloths; and accordingly we see some infant manufactures dispute the market with the produce of the greatest dexterity; the distaff dispute prices with the wheel. But when these provinces come to be purged of their superfluous mouths, spinning becomes a trade, and the spinners must live by it. Must not then prices naturally rise? And if these are not supported by the statesman, or if assistance is not given to these poor manufacturers, to enable them to increase their dexterity,

[1] Not included in these extracts.

in order to compensate what they are losing in cheapness, will not their industry fail? Will not the poor spinners be extinguished? For it is not to be expected, that the landlord will receive them back again from a principle of charity, after he has discovered their former uselessness.[1]

A third cause of a necessary augmentation upon the intrinsic value of goods proceeds from taxes. A statesman must be very negligent indeed, if he does not attend to the immediate consequences of his own proper operations. I shall not enlarge on this at present, as it would be an unnecessary anticipation; but I shall return, to resume the part of my reasoning which I broke off abruptly.

I have observed, how the same cause which stops the progress of industry, gives an encouragement to agriculture: how the rise in the price of subsistence necessarily increases the price of work to an industrious and well-employed people: how this cuts off a part of the demand for work, or sends it to a foreign market.

Now all these consequences are entirely just, and yet they seem contradictory to another part of my reasoning, (Book I. Chap. xvi)[2] where I set forth the advantages of a prodigal consumption of the earth's produce as advantageous to agriculture, by increasing the price of subsistence, without taking notice, on the other hand, of the hurt thereby done to industry, which supports the consumption of that produce.

The one and the other chain of consequences is equally just, and they appear contradictory only upon the supposition, that there is no statesman at the helm. These contradictions represent the alternate overturn of the balance. The duty of the statesman is, to support the double competition every where, and to permit only the gentle alternate vibrations of the two scales.

When the progress of industry has augmented numbers, and made subsistence scarce, he must estimate to what height it is expedient that the price of subsistence should rise. If he finds, that, in order to encourage the breaking up of new lands, the price of it must rise too high, and stand high too long, to preserve the intrinsic value of goods at the same standard as

[1] The original has 'usefulness', which is clearly an error.
[2] Not included in these extracts.

formerly; then he must assist agriculture with his purse, in order that exportation may not be discouraged. This will have the effect of increasing subsistence, according to the true proportion of the augmentation required, without raising the price of it too high. And if that operation be the work of time, and the demand for the augmentation be pressing, he must have subsistence imported, or brought from abroad, during that interval. This supply he may cut off whenever he pleases, that is, whenever it ceases to be necessary.

If the supply comes from a sister country, it must be so taken, as to occasion no violent revolution when it comes to be interrupted a-new. As for example: One province demands a supply of grain from another, only for a few years, until their own soil can be improved, so as to provide them sufficiently. The statesman should encourage agriculture, no doubt, in the province furnishing, and let the farmers know the extent of the demand, and the time it may probably last, as near as possible; but he must discourage the plucking up of vineyards, and even perhaps the breaking up of great quantities of old pasture; because, upon the ceasing of the demand, such changes upon the agriculture of the province furnishing, may occasion a hurtful revolution.

While this foreign supply is allowed to come in, the statesman should be closely employed in giving such encouragement to agriculture at home, according to the principles hereafter to be deduced,[1] as may nearly balance the discouragement given to it by this newly permitted importation. If this step be neglected, the consequence may be, that the foreign supply will go on increasing every year, and will extinguish the agriculture already established in the country, in place of supplying a temporary exigency, which is within the power of the country itself to furnish. These, I suppose, were the principles attended to by the government of England, upon opening their ports for the importation of provisions from Ireland.

The principle, therefore, being to support a gentle increase of food, inhabitants, work, and demand, the statesman must suffer small vibrations in the balance, which, by alternate competition, may favour both sides of the contract; but whenever

[1] Steuart deduces them mainly in Book II, Chapter xviii, not included in these extracts.

the competition stands too long upon either side, and threatens a subversion of the balance, then, with an artful hand, he must endeavour to load the lighter scale, and never, but in cases of the greatest necessity, have recourse to the expedient of taking any thing from the heaviest.

In treating of the present state of France, we observed, in the chapter above-cited,[1] how the vibration of the balance of agriculture and population may carry food and numbers to their height; but as foreign trade was not there the direct object of inquiry, I did not care to introduce this second balance of work and demand, for fear of perplexing my subject. I hope I have now abundantly shewn the force of the different principles, and it must depend upon the judgment of the statesman to combine them together, and adapt them to his plan: a thing impossible to be even chalked out by any person who is not immediately at the head of the affairs of a nation. My work resembles the formation of the pure colours for painting, it is the artist's business to mix them: all I can pretend to, is to reason consequentially from suppositions. If I go at any time farther, I exceed my plan, and I confess the fault.

I shall now conclude my chapter by introducing a new subject. I have been at pains to shew how the continued neglect of a statesman, in watching over the vibrations of the balance of work and demand, naturally produces a total subversion of it; but this is not, of itself, sufficient to undo an industrious people. Other nations must be taught to profit of the disorder; and this is what I call the competition between nations.

[1] Book I, Chapter xviii.

Josiah Tucker

THE FIRST TRACT FROM
FOUR TRACTS, ON POLITICAL
AND COMMERCIAL SUBJECTS
(1774)

Source: The text used is that of the third edition (1776), pp. vii and 17–56. Certain passages in the tract—which are noted at the appropriate points in the text—have been omitted. All the footnotes are the present editor's.

Josiah Tucker (1712–99), Dean of Gloucester and later of Bristol, was an indefatigable pamphleteer whose 'Mercantilism' (if one can call it that) was of a relatively liberal and enlightened type. The tract which forms our final reading is of interest not only in its own right, but also because it was the subject of an important exchange of views with David Hume in 1758.

In his essay *Of Money*, first published in 1752, Hume had argued that the advantages possessed by a rich country in trade

> are compensated, in some measure, by the low price of labour in every nation which has not an extensive commerce, and does not much abound in gold and silver. Manufactures, therefore gradually shift their places, leaving those countries and provinces which they have already enriched, and flying to others, whither they are allured by the cheapness of provisions and labour; till they have enriched these also, and are again banished by the same causes. And, in general, we may observe, that the dearness of every thing, from plenty of money, is a disadvantage, which attends an established commerce, and sets bounds to it in every country, by enabling the poorer states to undersel the richer in all foreign markets.[1]

Tucker, who had opened a correspondence with Lord Kames in 1757, seems shortly afterwards to have sent him some papers —presumably including a version of the present tract—which contained a critique of Hume's position on this point. Hume wrote a letter to Kames on 4 March 1758 setting out his answers to Tucker's criticisms;[2] and Tucker replied to Hume's 'ingenious animadversions' in a letter to Kames dated 6 July

---

[1] *Essays Moral, Political, and Literary by David Hume* (ed. T. H. Green and T. H. Grose, 1889) Vol. I, p. 311.

[2] Hume's 'objections' in this letter were later summarized by Tucker in the 'Postscript' to the tract: see below, pp. 191–2.

1758.[1] Tucker claimed in the preface to his *Four Tracts* that his arguments had converted Hume, or at any rate 'that in his Publications since our Correspondence, he has wrote, and reasoned, as if he was a Convert' (below, p. 177). Up to a point, Tucker's claim seems to have been justified: Hume, in an essay *Of the Jealousy of Trade* which he added to the others in a new edition published later in 1758, argued that because of the 'diversity of geniuses, climates, and soils' in different nations no state need fear 'that their neighbours will improve to such a degree in every art and manufacture, as to have no demand from them'.[2] Indeed, in one respect Tucker's arguments succeeded—from his point of view—only too well, in that Hume in his 1758 essay advanced much further towards the pure free trade position than Tucker would probably have considered prudent.[3]

Quite apart from all this, however, a number of Tucker's arguments in the tract are interesting as anticipations of certain elements in the Smithian 'paradigm'. Smith, it is true, would not have accepted Tucker's proposition (below, pp. 179–80) that there could not possibly be any real conflict between 'our *Duty*' and 'our *Interest*' because the Almighty would not permit it—or at any rate Smith would not have accepted it in this form, and within so overtly theological an integument. But the implied distinction between 'productive' and 'unproductive' labour in Tucker's consideration of his 'Case I' has a distinctly Smithian flavour, and the Edinburgh illustration (p. 183) reappears, in very similar language, in the *Wealth of Nations*.[4] And in the latter part of the tract a whole number of 'Smithian' ideas are to be found in embryo. Conspicuous among these are the division of labour, duly limited by the extent of the market (p. 186); the idea that 'Heaps of Gold and

---

[1] Tucker's arguments were repeated and elaborated in the latter part of the 'Postscript' to the tract: see below, pp. 192–6.

[2] *Essays Moral, Political, and Literary by David Hume*, Vol. I, p. 346.

[3] Eugene Rotwein, in *David Hume: Writings on Economics* (1955), publishes the relevant parts of the Tucker–Kames–Hume correspondence, and makes some interesting comments on the issues involved (pp. lix, lxxvii, and 199–205).

[4] *Wealth of Nations* (ed. E. Cannan, 1904, 6th edn., 1950), Vol. I, p. 358.

Silver are not the True Riches of a Nation' (p. 189); the notion of the crucial importance of capital, both fixed and circulating, and the advantages accruing from the possession of 'superior Capitals' (pp. 184–7); the idea that in a rich country monopoly is ousted by competition, which lowers prices (p. 187); and even, in one place, a concept of profit on capital which, with the exercise of a little charity, may be regarded as not essentially dissimilar to Smith's (p. 187).

Finally, mention should be made of Tucker's very interesting discussion of the general idea of progress (below, pp. 192 and 195–6), which was stimulated by Hume's statement, in his letter to Kames of 4 March 1758, that 'great empires, great cities, great commerce, all of them receive a check, not from accidental events, but necessary principles'. Tucker's much more optimistic view is expressed more cautiously than Turgot's was, but more explicitly than Smith's was, and constitutes a significant formulation of the British (as distinct from the French) version of the doctrine of progress which was associated with the Enlightenment.

FOUR TRACTS, ON POLITICAL AND COMMERCIAL SUBJECTS

FROM THE PREFACE

The first of these Pieces was never printed before, and is now published as a Kind of Introduction to those that follow, or as a Sort of Basis on which the succeeding Arguments are chiefly founded. The Piece itself arose from a Correspondence in the Year 1758, with a Gentleman of *North-Britain*, eminently distinguished in the Republic of Letters.[1] Though I cannot boast that I had the Honour of making the Gentleman a *declared* Convert, yet I can say, and prove likewise, that in his Publications since our Correspondence, he has wrote, and reasoned, as if he was a Convert. . . .

[1] David Hume. See above, pp. 175–6.

TRACT I

*The great Question resolved, Whether a rich Country can stand a
Competition with a poor Country (of equal natural Advantages)
in raising of Provisions, and Cheapness of Manufactures?—With
suitable Inferences and Deductions.*

IT has been a Notion universally received, That Trade and
Manufactures, if left at *full Liberty*, will always descend from a
richer to a poorer State; somewhat in the same Manner as a
Stream of Water falls from higher to lower Grounds; or as a
Current of Air rushes from a heavier to a lighter Part of the
Atmosphere, in order to restore the Equilibrium. It is likewise
inferred, very consistently with this first Principle, that when
the poor Country, in Process of Time, and by this Influx of
Trade and Manufactures, is become relatively richer, the
Course of Traffic will turn again: So that by attending to this
Change, you may discover the comparative Riches or Poverty
of each particular Place or Country.

THE Reasons usually assigned for this Migration, or rather
Circulation of Industry and Commerce, are the following, *viz.*
In rich Countries, where Money is Plenty, a greater Quantity
thereof is given for all the Articles of Food, Raiment, and
Dwelling: Whereas in poor Countries, where Money is scarce,
a lesser Quantity of it is made to serve in procuring the like
Necessaries of Life, and in paying the Wages of the Shepherd,
the Plowman, the Artificer, and Manufacturer. The Inference
from all which is, that Provisions are raised, and Goods manufactured much cheaper in poor Countries than in rich ones;
and therefore every poor Country, if a near Neighbour to a rich
one, and if there is an easy and commodious Communication
between them, must unavoidably get the Trade from it,—were
Trade to be left at Liberty to take its natural Course. Nor will
this Increase of Agriculture and Manufactures, whereby the
richer Country is drained, and the poorer proportionably
enriched, be stopped or prevented, 'till Things are brought to a
perfect Level, or the Tide of Wealth begins to turn the other
Way.

Now, according to this Train of Reasoning, one alarming and
obvious Consequence must necessarily follow, *viz.* That the

Provisions and Manufactures of a rich Country could never find a Vent in a poor one, on Account of the higher Value, or dearer Price set upon them: Whereas those of a poor Country would always find a Vent in a rich one, because they would be afforded the cheapest at the common Market.

THIS being the Case, can it be denied, that every poor Country is the natural and unavoidable Enemy of a rich one; especially if it should happen to be adjoining to it? And are not we sure beforehand, that it will never cease from draining it of its Trade and Commerce, Industry and Manufactures, 'till it has reduced it, at least so far as to be on a Level and Equality with itself? Therefore the rich Country, if it regards its own Interest, is obliged by a Kind of Self-defence to make War upon the poor one, and to endeavour to extirpate all its Inhabitants, in order to maintain itself in *statu quo*, or to prevent the fatal Consequences of losing its present Influence, Trade and Riches. For little less than a total Extirpation can be sufficient to guard against the Evils to be feared from this dangerous Rival, while it is suffered to exist.

BUT is this indeed the Case?—One would not willingly run counter to the settled Notions of Mankind; and yet one ought not to make a Sacrifice of Truth to mere Numbers, and the Authority of Opinion; especially if it should appear that these are Truths of great Moment to the Welfare of Society. Therefore, with a becoming Deference, may it not here be asked,— Can you suppose that Divine Providence has really constituted the Order of Things in such a Sort, as to make the Rule of national Self-Preservation to be inconsistent with the fundamental Principle of universal Benevolence, and the doing as we would be done by? For my Part, I must confess, I never could conceive that an all-wise, just, and benevolent Being would contrive one Part of his Plan to be so contradictory to the other, as here supposed;—that is, would lay us under one Obligation as to Morals, and another as to Trade; or, in short, make that to be our *Duty*, which is not, upon the whole, and generally speaking (even without the Consideration of a future State) our *Interest* likewise.

THEREFORE I conclude *a priori*, that there must be some Flaw or other in the preceding Arguments, plausible as they seem, and great as they are upon the Foot of human Authority.

For though the Appearance of Things at first Sight makes for this Conclusion, *viz.* 'That poor Countries must inevitably draw away the Trade from rich ones, and consequently impoverish them,' the Fact itself CANNOT BE SO. But leaving all Arguments of this Sort, as being perhaps too metaphysical for common Use, let us have Recourse to others, wherein we may be assisted by daily Experience and Observation.

SUPPOSE therefore *England* and *Scotland* to be two contiguous, independant Kingdoms, equal in Size, Situation, and all natural Advantages; suppose likewise, that the Numbers of People in both were nearly equal; but that *England* had acquired TWENTY MILLIONS of current Specie, and *Scotland* had only a tenth Part of that Sum, *viz.* TWO MILLIONS: The Question now is, Whether *England* will be able to support itself in its superior Influence, Wealth, and Credit? Or be continually on the Decline in Trade and Manufactures, 'till it is sunk into a Parity with *Scotland;* so that the current Specie of both Nations will be brought to be just the same, *viz. Eleven Millions* each.

Now, to resolve this Question in a satisfactory Manner, a previous Enquiry should be set on Foot, *viz.* How came *England* to acquire this great Surplus of Wealth? And by what Means was it accumulated?—If in the Way of *Idleness*, it certainly cannot retain it long; and *England* will again become poor;—perhaps so poor as to be little better than *Hungary* or *Poland:* But if by a Course of *regular and universal Industry*, the same Means, which obtained the Wealth at first, will, *if pursued*, certainly preserve it, and even add thereto: So that *England* need not entertain any Jealousy against the Improvements and Manufactures of *Scotland;*—and on the other Hand, *Scotland* without hurting *England*, will likewise increase in Trade, and be benefited both by its Example, and its Riches.

BUT as these are only general Assertions, let us now endeavour to support them by an Induction of particular Cases.

CASE I.

ENGLAND has acquired 20,000,000l. of Specie in the Way of *National Idleness*, *viz.* Either by Discoveries of very rich Mines

of Gold and Silver,—or by successful Privateering and making
Captures of Plate Ships, —or by the Trade of Jewels, and
vending them to foreign Nations for vast Sums of Money,—
or, in short, by any other conceivable Method, wherein
(universal Industry and Application being out of the Question)
very few Hands were employed in getting this Mass of Wealth
(and they only by Fits and Starts, not constantly)—and fewer
still are supposed to retain what is gotten.

ACCORDING to this State of the Case, it seems evidently to
follow, That the Provisions and Manufactures of such a Country would bear a most enormous Price, while this Flush of
Money lasted; and that for the two following Reasons: 1st.
A People enriched by such improper Means as these, would
not know the real Value of Money, but would give any Price
that was asked; their superior Folly and Extravagance being
the only Evidence which they could produce of their superior
Riches. 2dly. At the same Time that Provisions and Manufactures would bear such an excessive Price, the Quantity thereof
raised or made within the Kingdom would be less than ever;
inasmuch as the Cart, and the Plow, the Anvil, the Wheel, and
the Loom, would certainly be laid aside for these quicker and
easier Arts of getting rich, and becoming fine Gentlemen and
Ladies; because all Persons, whether male or female, would
endeavour to put themselves in Fortune's Way, and hope to
catch as much as they could of this golden Shower. Hence the
Number of Coaches, Post-Chaises, and all other Vehicles of
Pleasure, would prodigiously increase; while the usual Sets of
Farmer's Carts and Waggons proportionably decreased: The
Sons of lower Tradesmen and Labourers would be converted
into spruce, powdered Footmen; and that robust Breed, which
used to supply the Calls for laborious Occupations, and
common Manufactures, would turn off to commence Barbers
and Hair-Dressers, Dancing-Masters, Players, Fidlers, Pimps,
and Gamesters. As to the Female Sex, it is no difficult Matter
to foresee, what would be the Fate of the younger, the more
sprightly, and pleasing Part among them. In short, the whole
People would take a new Turn; and while Agriculture, and the
ordinary mechanic Trades became shamefully neglected, the
Professions which subsist by procuring Amusements and
Diversions, and exhibiting Allurements and Temptations,

would be amazingly increased,—and indeed for a Time enriched; so that from being a Nation of Bees producing Honey, they would become a Nation of Drones to eat it up. In such a Case certain it is, that their industrious Neighbours would soon drain them of this Quantity of Specie,—and not only drain them, so far as to reduce them to a Level with the poor Country, but also sink them into the lowest State of abject Poverty. Perhaps indeed some few of the Inhabitants, being naturally Misers, and foreseeing the general Poverty that was coming upon the Country, would make the more ample Provision for themselves; and, by feeding the Vices, and administering to the Follies and Extravagances of others, would amass and engross great Estates. Therefore when such a Nation came to awake out of this gilded Dream, it would find itself to be much in the same Circumstances of pretended Wealth, but real Poverty, as the *Spaniards* and *Portuguese* are at present. Nay, when their Mines, or their former Resources of Gold and Silver, came to fail them, they would really be in a much worse; and their Condition would then approach the nearest of any Thing we can now conceive, to that of Baron and Vassal in *Poland* and *Hungary*, or to Planter and Slave in the *West Indies*.

[A paragraph dealing with certain aspects of ' the Expedition in the late Spanish *War against* Carthagena' *is omitted at this point.]*

HENCE likewise we may discern the Weakness of one Argument (indeed the only popular one) sometimes insisted on with more Warmth than Judgment in Favour of a general Naturalization, *viz.* That it would induce such rich Foreigners as are not engaged in any Trade or Business, and consequently would not interfere with any of the Natives, to come and *spend their Fortunes* in this Land of Liberty. [What is truly to be hoped from a general Naturalization, is, that it would induce industrious and ingenious Foreigners, Men who have their Fortunes yet to make, to come, and enrich the Country at the same Time that they are enriching themselves by their superior Industry, Ingenuity, and other good Qualities.] For as to idle Foreigners, living on the Income of their great Estates,—pray, of what national Advantage would they be to us? What, I say, even supposing we could persuade all the wealthy Foreigners of this Class throughout the World to come and reside in *England*? The real Fact is, that no other Consequences could ensue, but that this Nation, instead of being chiefly composed of substantial Yeomen, and Farmers, creditable Manufacturers, and opulent Merchants, would then become a Nation of Gentlemen and Ladies on the one Side, and of Footmen and Grooms, Ladies' Women, and Laundresses, and such like Dependants, on the other. In short we have Proofs enough already of this Matter, now before our Eyes, and in our own Kingdom, if we will but make the proper Use of them. For Example, the Towns of *Birmingham*, *Leeds*, *Halifax*, *Manchester*, *&c. &c.* being inhabited in a Manner altogether by Tradesmen and Manufacturers, are some of the richest and most flourishing in the Kingdom: Whereas the City of *York*, and such other Places as seem to be more particularly set apart for the Residence of Persons who live upon their Fortunes, are not without evident Marks of Poverty and Decay.

HENCE also we come to the true Reason, why the City of *Edinburgh*, contrary to the Fears and Apprehensions of its Inhabitants, has thriven and flourished more since the Union than it did before, *viz*. It has lost the Residence of the Court and Parliament, and has got in its Stead, Commerce and Manufactures; that is, it has exchanged Idleness for Industry: And were the Court and Parliament of *Ireland* to leave *Dublin* by Virtue of an Union with *Great-Britain*, the same good Consequences would certainly follow.

CASE II.

ENGLAND has acquired TWENTY MILLIONS of Specie in the Way of *general industry*, *viz*. By exciting the Ingenuity and Activity of its People, and giving them a free Scope without any Exclusion, Confinement, or Monopoly;—by annexing Burdens to Celibacy, and Honours and Privileges to the married State; —by constituting such Laws, as diffuse the Wealth of the Parents more equally among the Children, than the present Laws of *Europe* generally do;—by modelling the Taxes in such a Manner, that all Things hurtful to the Publick Good shall be rendered proportionably dear, and placed beyond the Reach of the Multitude; whereas such Things as are necessary, or useful, shall be proportionably encouraged; and, in short, by every other conceivable Method, whereby the Drones of Society may be converted into Bees, and the Bees be prevented from degenerating back into Drones.

THEREFORE, as we are to suppose, that by such Means as these, the *South-Britons* have accumulated 20,000,000l. in Specie, while the *North Britons* have no more than 2,000,000l.: The Question now is, Which of these two Nations can afford to raise Provisions, and sell their Manufactures on the cheapest Terms? 'Supposing that both did their utmost to rival one another, and that Trade and Manufactures were left at Liberty to take their own Course, according as Cheapness or Interest directed them.'

Now, on the Side of the poorer Nation, it is alleged, That seeing it hath much less Money, and yet is equal in Size, Situation, and other natural Advantages, equal also in Numbers of People, and those equally willing to be diligent and industrious; it cannot be but that such a Country must have a manifest Advantage over the rich one in Point of its parsimonious Way of Living, low Wages, and consequently cheap Manufactures.

ON the contrary, the rich Country hath the following Advantages which will more than counter-ballance any Disadvantage that may arise from the foregoing Articles, *viz.*

1st. As the richer Country hath acquired its superior Wealth by a general Application, and long Habits of Industry, it is therefore in actual Possession of an established Trade and Credit, large Correspondences, experienced Agents and Factors, commodious Shops, Work-Houses, Magazines, *&c.* also a great Variety of the best Tools and Implements in the various Kinds of Manufactures, and Engines for abridging Labour;—add to these good Roads, Canals, and other artificial Communications; Quays, Docks, Wharfs, and Piers; Numbers of Ships, good Pilots, and trained Sailors:—And in respect to Husbandry and Agriculture, it is likewise in Possession of good Enclosures, Drains, Waterings, artificial Grasses, great Stocks, and consequently the greater Plenty of Manures; also a great

Variety of Plows, Harrows, &c. suited to the different Soils; and in short of every other superior Method of Husbandry arising from long Experience, various and expensive Trials. Whereas the poor Country has, for the most Part, all these Things to seek after and procure.—Therefore what the Poet observed to be true in a private Sense, is true also in a public and commercial one, viz.

> Haud facile emergunt, quorum virtutibus obstat
> Res angusta domi—[1]

2dly. THE richer Country is not only in Possession of the Things already made and settled, but also of superior Skill and Knowledge (acquired by long Habit and Experience) for inventing and making of more. The Importance of this will appear the greater, when we consider that no Man can pretend to set Bounds to the Progress that may yet be made both in Agriculture and Manufactures; for who can take upon him to affirm, that our Children cannot as far exceed us as we have exceeded our Gothic Forefathers? And is it not much more natural and reasonable to suppose, that we are rather at the Beginning only, and just got within the Threshold, than that we are arrived at the *ne plus ultra* of useful Discoveries? Now, if so, the poorer Country, however willing to learn, cannot be supposed to be capable of making the same Progress in Learning with the Rich, for want of equal Means of Instruction, equally good Models and Examples;—and therefore, tho' both may be improving every Day, yet the *practical* Knowledge of the poorer in Agriculture and Manufactures will always be found to keep at a respectful Distance behind that of the richer Country.

3dly. THE richer Country is not only more *knowing*, but is also more able than the other to make further Improvements, by laying out large Sums of Money in the Prosecution of the intended Plan. Whereas the poor Country has here again the Mortification to find, that the *Res angusta domi* is in many Cases an insuperable Bar to its Rise and Advancement: And this Circumstance deserves the more Regard as it is a known Fact and trite Observation, that very few great and extensive

---

[1] 'It is no easy matter for a man to rise when poverty stands in the way of his merits' (Juvenal, *Satire III*, lines 164–5).

Projects were ever brought to bear at first setting out; and that a vast deal of Money must be sunk, and many Years be elapsed, before they are capable of making any Returns. In short, the Inhabitants of a poor Country, who, according to the vulgar Phrase, generally live from Hand to Mouth, *dare not* make such costly Experiments, or embark in such expensive and long-winded Undertakings, as the Inhabitants of a rich Country can attempt, and execute with Ease.

4thly. THE higher Wages of the rich Country, and the greater Scope and Encouragement given for the Exertion of Genius, Industry, and Ambition, will naturally determine a great many Men of Spirit and Enterprize to forsake their own poor Country, and settle in the richer; so that the one will always drain the other of the Flower of its Inhabitants: Whereas there are not the same Temptations for the best Hands and Artists of a rich Country to forsake the best Pay, and settle in a poor one. —Though for Argument's Sake, it was allowed at the Beginning, that the Numbers of People in these two adjoining States were just equal, yet certain it is, that the Thing itself could never have so happened,—the richer Country being always endowed with the attractive Quality of the Loadstone, and the poor one with the repelling: And therefore, seeing that the poorer Country must necessarily be the least peopled (if there is a free Intercourse between them) the Consequence would be, that in several Districts, and in many Instances, it would be impossible for certain Trades even to subsist; because the Scarcity and Poverty of the Inhabitants would not afford a sufficient Number of Customers to frequent the Shop, or to take off the Goods of the Manufacturer.

5thly. IN the richer Country, where the Demands are great and constant, every Manufacture that requires various Processes, and is composed of different Parts, is accordingly divided and subdivided into separate and distinct Branches; whereby each Person becomes more expert, and also more expeditious in the particular Part assigned him. Whereas in a poor Country, the same Person is obliged by Necessity, and for the Sake of getting a bare Subsistence, to undertake such different Branches, as prevent him from excelling, or being expeditious in any. In such a Case, Is it not much cheaper to give 2s. 6d. a Day in the rich Country to the nimble and adroit Artist, than it is to give only 6d. in the poor one, to the tedious, aukward Bungler?

6thly. As the richer Country has the greater Number of rival Tradesmen, and those more quick and dexterous, the Goods of such a Country have not only the Advantages arising from Quickness and Dexterity, but also will be afforded much the cheaper on Account of the Emulation of so many Rivals and Competitors. Whereas in a poor Country, it is very easy for one rich, over-grown Tradesman to monopolize the whole Trade to himself, and consequently to set his own Price upon the Goods, as he knows that there are none who dare contend with him in Point of Fortune;—or, what is full as bad, the like Consequences will follow where the Numbers of the Wealthy are so few, that they can combine together whenever they will, to prey upon the Public.

7thly. and lastly. IN the rich Country, the Superiority of the Capital, and the low Interest of Money, will insure the vending of all Goods on the cheapest Terms; because a Man of 2000l. Capital can certainly afford to give the best Wages to the best Workmen, and yet be able to sell the Produce or Manufacture of such Workmen at a much cheaper Rate than he who has only a Capital of 200l. For if the one gets only 10l. per Cent. per Ann. for his Money, that will bring him an Income of 200l. a Year; a Sum very sufficient to live with Credit and Reputation in the Rank of a Tradesman, and considerably more than double to what he would have received in the Way of common Interest, even if lent at 4l. and a Half per Cent. Whereas, the other with his poor Capital of 200l. must get a Profit of at least 20l. per Cent. in order to have an Income just above the Degree of a common Journeyman.—Not to mention, that Men of superior Capitals will always command the Market in buying the raw Materials at the best Hand; and command it also in another View, *viz.* by being able to give longer Credit to their Dealers and Customers.—So much as to the reasoning Part of this Subject: Let us now examine how stand the Facts.

AND here it must be premised, that were a greater Quantity of Specie to enhance the Price of Provisions and Manufactures in the Manner usually supposed, the Consequence would be, that all Goods whatever would be so much the dearer in a rich Country, compared with a poor one, as there had been different

Sets of People employed, and greater Wages paid in making them. For the Argument proceeds thus,—The more Labour, the more Wages;—the more Wages, the more Money;—the more Money paid for making them, the dearer the Goods must come to Market: And yet the Fact itself is quite the Reverse of this seemingly just Conclusion. For it may be laid down as a general Proposition, which very seldom fails, That *operose* or *complicated Manufactures* are cheapest in rich Countries;—and *raw Materials* in poor ones: And therefore in Proportion as any Commodity approaches to one, or other of these *Extremes*, in that Proportion it will be found to be cheaper, or dearer in a rich, or a poor Country.

[Seven paragraphs containing practical illustrations of this proposition are omitted at this point.]

JUDGE now, therefore, what little Cause there is to fear that a poor Country can ever rival a rich one in the more operose, complicated, and expensive Branches of a Manufacture: Judge also, whether a rich Country can ever lose its Trade, while it retains its Industry; and consequently how absurd must every Project be for securing or encreasing this Trade, which doth not tend to secure, or encrease the Diligence and Frugality of the People.

A War, whether crowned with Victory, or branded with Defeats, can never prevent another Nation from being more industrious than you are; and if they are more industrious, they will sell cheaper; and consequently your former Customers will forsake your Shop, and go to theirs; tho' you covered the Ocean with Fleets, and the Land with Armies:—In short, the Soldier may lay Waste, the Privateer, whether, successful or unsuccessful, will make Poor; but it is the eternal Law of Providence, that *The Hand of the Diligent alone can make Rich.*

THIS being the Case, it evidently follows, that as no trading Nation can ever be ruined but by itself, so more particularly the Improvements and Manufactures of *Scotland* can never be a Detriment to *England;* unless the *English* do voluntarily decline their Industry, and become profligate in their Morals. Indeed when this comes to pass, it is of little Consequence by what Name that Nation is called, which runs away with their

Trade; for some Country or other necessarily must. Whereas, were the *English* to reform their Manners, and encrease their Industry, the very Largeness of their Capitals, and their Vicinity to *Scotland*, might enable the *English* to assist the *Scotch* in various Ways, without prejudicing themselves, *viz.* By lending them Money at moderate Interest,—by embarking in Partnership with them in such Undertakings as require large Stocks and long Credits,—by supplying them with Models and Instructors,—exciting their Emulation, and directing their Operations with that Judgment and good Order which are only learnt by Use and Experience.

NAY, to pass from Particulars to Generals, we may lay it down as an universal Rule, subject to very few Exceptions, that as an industrious Nation can never be hurt by the increasing Industry of its Neighbours; and as it is so wisely contrived by Divine Providence, that all People should have a strong Biass towards the Produce and Manufactures of others;—so it follows, that when this Biass is put under *proper Regulations*, the respective Industry of Nation and Nation enables them to be so much the better Customers, to improve in a friendly Intercourse, and to be a mutual Benefit to each other. A private Shopkeeper would certainly wish that his Customers did improve in their Circumstances, rather than go behind-hand; because every such Improvement would probably redound to his Advantage. Where then can be the Wisdom in the public Shopkeeper, a trading People, to endeavour to make the neighbouring States and Nations, that are his Customers, so very poor as not to be able to trade with him?

THE Conclusion of the whole is this: Heaps of Gold and Silver are not the true Riches of a Nation: Gold and Silver got in the Ways of Idleness are its certain Ruin; it is Wealth in Appearance but Poverty in Reality: Gold and Silver got by Industry, and spent in Idleness, will prove to be Destruction likewise: But Gold and Silver acquired by general Industry, and used with Sobriety, and according to good Morals, will promote still greater Industry, and go on, for any Thing that appears to the contrary, still accumulating; so that every Augmentation of such Money is a Proof of a preceding Increase of Industry: Whereas an Augmentation of Money by such Means as decrease Industry, is a national Curse—not a Blessing. And therefore, tho' the Accounts of such a Nation may look fair to the Eyes of a Merchant or Tradesman, who (keeping their own Books by Pounds, Shillings, and Pence) suppose, that all must be right, when they see at the Foot of the Account, a large Balance of Pounds, Shillings, and Pence, in the Nation's Favour; yet the able Statesman, and judicious Patriot, who are to keep the public Accounts by quite different Columns,— by Men, Women, and Children employed, or not employed,— will regard this Tumour of Wealth as a dangerous Disease, not as a natural and healthy Growth. In one Word, the only possible Means of preventing a Rival Nation from running away with your Trade, is to prevent your own People from being more idle and vicious than they are; and by inspiring them with the contrary good Qualities: So that the only War, which can be attended with Success in that Respect, is a War against Vice and Idleness; a War, whose Forces must consist of —not Fleets and Armies,—but such judicious Taxes and wise Regulations, as shall turn the Passion of private Self-Love into the Channel of public Good. Indeed Fleets and Armies may be necessary, where the Merchant and Manufacturer are in Danger of being robbed or plundered in carrying their Goods to Market; but Fleets and Armies can never render those Goods the cheaper; and consequently cannot possibly encrease the Number of their Customers; supposing such Customers have the Liberty of trading wherever they please, and to the best Advantage. But if you should continue these Armaments, in order to stop up the Ports of other Nations, and deprive them of the Benefit of a free Trade, what will be the Consequence of this *wise* Manœuvre? Plainly this;—That while you are getting One Shilling, you are spending Ten; while you are employing a few in a Course of regular Industry, you are supporting Thousands in Habits of Idleness, and at the same Time involving the Nation in such immense Expences as must, if persisted in, inevitably prove its Ruin.—Grant, therefore, that during a War, a War crowned with *uninterrupted* Success (for no other can avail) grant, I say, that in some Articles you enjoy an Increase of Trade, at what Expence is this Increase obtained, and how long is it to last? Moreover, what Consequences will arise when the War is at an End, and other Ports are open? (for surely it cannot be intended that a trading Nation is to fight for ever,) and when Peace is made, what new Duties, what additional Taxes are to be imposed for defraying both Principal and Interest of the Charges of such a War?—How are they to be levied?—Who is to bear them?—And will you by this Means be better able to render your Goods cheaper at a foreign Market than heretofore?—A plain Answer to these Questions would unravel the whole Matter, and bring Mankind to a right Use of their Senses.

POSTSCRIPT TO THE TRACT[1]

THE only Set of Objections, as far as they have come to my Knowledge, which have been hitherto made to the Principles and Reasonings laid down and illustrated in the foregoing Treatise, are the following:

1st. THAT according to this Hypothesis, Improvements, Industry, and Riches, may be advanced and increased *ad infinitum;* which is a Position too extravagant to be admitted.

2dly. THAT in Consequence of this accumulating Scheme, one Nation might engross the Trade of the whole World, and beggar every other State or Kingdom; which Opinion is not only contradicted by Fact and Experience, but is also contrary to my own System of Commerce, wherein I strongly declare against Monopoly and Exclusion of every Kind.

3dly. THAT tho' a poor Country cannot immediately and at once rival a rich one in its Trade and Manufactures, yet it may do it by Degrees, beginning first with the coarser and less complicated Kinds, and then advancing Step by Step to others more compounded, operose, and costly; 'till at length it hath reached *that* Summit of Art, Industry, and Riches, from which the rich Country hath lately fallen, and from whence also this upstart Adventurer must recede in its Turn. And to strengthen this Reasoning it may be observed,

4thly. 'That all human Things have the Seeds of Decay within themselves:—Great Empires, great Cities, great Com-

---

[1] The four 'objections' dealt with in this postscript were made by David Hume in a letter to Lord Kames of 4 March 1758. See above, p. 175.

merce, all of them receive a Cheque, not from accidental Events, but from necessary Principles.'[1]

THUS stand the Objections of that acute Philosopher, and celebrated Writer, who honoured the above Treatise with his ingenious Remarks. Let us now therefore attend to the Force of each of these Objections with that Care and Impartiality which the Cause of Truth deserves; and with that Respect also, which is due to a Person of Eminence in the Republic of Letters.

AND 1st. I must beg Leave to observe, that the Gentleman has, in Part at least, mistaken my Meaning, where I say, towards the Close of the Treatise, 'That Gold and Silver acquired by *general* Industry, and used with Sobriety, and according to good Morals, will promote still greater Industry, and go on, for any Thing that appears to the contrary, still accumulating:'—I say he has mistaken my Meaning, if he imagined, that I roundly and positively there asserted, that the Progress *must be, ad infinitum:* For I did not intend to assert any such Thing, and one Reason, among others, which restrained me, was the Consideration that I am not Metaphysician enough to comprehend what INFINITY really means. Therefore what I undertake to maintain, is this,—That such a Progression, as is here described, may be so far carried on, as evidently to prove, that no Man can positively define, *when* or *where* it must *necessarily* stop: No Man can set Bounds to Improvements even in Imagination: and therefore, 'till the *ne plus ultra* of all Advancements in Arts, Sciences, and Manufactures, in Agriculture, Trade, and Navigation, *&c. &c.* is clearly demonstrated (a Thing which I presume no one will be in Haste to attempt) we may still be allowed to assert, that the richer manufacturing Nation will maintain its Superiority over the poorer one, notwithstanding this latter may be likewise advancing towards Perfection. This being the Cause it follows.

2dly. THAT my Hypothesis is so far from supposing that one Nation may engross the Trade of the whole World, and beggar

[1] cf. Hume, loc. cit.: ' . . . The growth of all bodies, artificial as well as natural, is stopped by internal causes, derived from their enormous size and greatness. Great empires, great cities, great commerce, all of them receive a check, not from accidental events, but necessary principles.'

all the rest, that it remains just the contrary: Because it follows, from my System, that every Nation, poor as well as rich, may improve their Condition if they please. The poorer Nation for Example, may adopt the good Police,—the Abolition of Monopolies and exclusive Companies, and several useful Regulations of its richer neighbouring State: All these it may adopt *without Expence*, at the same Time that it may avoid their Errors or Mistakes; for Errors there will be, more or less, in all human Institutions. Moreover, tho' the poorer Nation cannot rival the Manufactures of a richer one at a third Place, or in a foreign Market, where the Goods and Merchandize of both are supposed to be admissible on the same Footing, yet it may, and ought, by Means of judicious Taxes, to discourage the too great or excessive Consumption of alien Manufactures, and especially Liquors, within its own Territories; and as this likewise may be done *without Expence*, nay, to the great Advantage of the Revenue, it therefore follows, that the poorer Nation may get forwards in many Respects without being obstructed by the rich one. To which Consideration we should not forget to add, that there are certain *local* Advantages resulting either from the Climate, the Soil, the Productions, the Situation, or even the natural Turn and peculiar Genius of one People preferably to those of another, which no Nation can deprive another of, unless by Violence and Conquest; and therefore, these being out of the Question, the necessary Consequence is, that the poor Country is left at Liberty to cultivate all these natural and local Advantages, as far as it can. Nay, I observe further, that the very superior Riches of a neighbouring State may contribute greatly to the carrying of such a Plan into Execution: And here I do not mean merely to say, that the Manufacturers and Merchant Adventurers of the poorer Country may avail themselves of the Wealth of a richer by borrowing Money, at a low Interest, to be employed in Trade; tho' by the bye, that is no small Benefit: But what I lay the chief Stress on at present is, *that a rich Neighbour is more likely to become a good Customer than a poor one;* and consequently, that the Traders of the poorer Country will find a better Market, and a more general Demand for their *peculiar* Productions, whether of Art or Nature, by Means of the superior Wealth and great Consumptions of their richer Neighbours, than they could possibly have had, were the latter equally poor with themselves. Moreover, *vice versa*, I affirm on the other Hand, that even the rich Country will be benefited in its Turn, by this Accession of Wealth flowing into the poor one. For when the Inhabitants of a poorer Country feel themselves *enabled*, there is no Doubt to be made, but that they will become also proportionably willing to purchase some of the more commodious or more sumptuous Furniture, and elegant Manufactures, of those Persons, who are actually their best Customers, as well as richer Neighbours. Indeed, to say the Truth, these Things are no other than the useful Consequences, and almost necessary Effects of natural Causes: And surely that Man must have been a very great Stranger to what passes in the World, who cannot discern these daily Rotations of Commercial Industry.

BUT there is one Circumstance more, relative to this Subject, which being not so obvious to common Observers, seems therefore to require a particular Explanation. The Circumstance is this,—That the very same Country may be relatively both richer and poorer than another at the very same Time, if considered in different Points of View; and consequently, that all the opposite and seemingly contradictory Assertions concerning both the Cheapness and Dearness of Manufactures, may be found to correspond with Truth and Matters of Fact. Thus, for Example, *England* is undoubtedly richer either than *Scotland* or *Ireland*, in regard to most Branches of Trade and Manufactures; and therefore it sells those Manufactures much cheaper than they can be fabricated in either of those Countries. But nevertheless, both *Scotland* and *Ireland* are richer than *England* in respect to one particular Point; for both these Countries have got the Start of *England* with respect to the *Linen Manufacture*, by more than Half a Century; and in Consequence thereof, their Capitals are larger, their Machinery is better, and their Correspondences are become more extensive; so that in short, almost every Thing relative to the Linen Manufacture in those Countries is conducted with more Adroitness, and managed to greater Advantage than in *England*. Hence therefore it is easily to be accounted for, how it comes to pass that the *Scotch* and *Irish* can sell their Linens, and more especially their fine Linens, considerably cheaper than the

English Linen Manufacturer is able to do. Nay, by Way of strengthening the general Argument, I would observe further, that tho' the Modes of Living are more expensive, tho' the daily Wages, and Rents of Houses and Lands, and the Prices of Provisions, are at least *doubled*, if not *trebled*, in the manufacturing Parts of *Scotland* and *Ireland*, to what they were about 60 or 70 Years ago,—yet the present Linens are both better and cheaper than the former, in a very considerable Degree; so that THE *Scotland* and *Ireland* of the Year 1763, if compared with THE *Scotland* or *Ireland* of 1700, are as strong an Instance, and as convincing a Proof, as can possibly be desired of the Truth of these Positions:—And hence also ¦we may observe, that the Riches of *England* in *many* Branches, and the Riches of *Scotland* and *Ireland* in *some* Branches, are mutually assistant to, and reciprocally advantageous to each other: For by mutually consuming and wearing each other's Manufactures, the *English*, *Scotch*, and *Irish*, become the better and the greater Customers to each other.

THE 3d Objection needs not a Reply so long and laboured as the second: For when the Gentleman proposed, that the poorer Country should first begin with the coarser and more simple Manufactures, and then proceed Step by Step to others more operose, complicated, and expensive, 'till at last it had supplanted the rich one in all its Trade and Manufactures,—he unfortunately forgot, that in Proportion as his poorer Country made a Progress in these Things, in the same Proportion, or nearly the same, would the Price of Labour, of Provisions, and of raw Materials, advance likewise; so that all these imaginary advantages would vanish away like a Dream, when they were most wanted, and when he most depended on their Assistance. In fact, his not paying due Attention to this Circumstance was probably the very Thing which led him and others into so many Errors on this Head. But as he had one Objection more to offer, let us see whether the Weight of that will make up for the Deficiency of the others.

Now his 4th Objection, or rather his Observation is, 'That all human Things have the Seeds of Decay within themselves: Great Empires, great Cities, great Commerce, all of them receive a Check, not from accidental Events, but from necessary Principles.' From all which it is implied, that the richer Nation cannot maintain its Superiority over a poorer one; because when it comes to a certain Period, it must necessarily fall to Decay;—I say, this must be the Inference intended, otherwise the Observation is not applicable, and has nothing to do with the present Subject.

HERE therefore, as the Ideas and Terms made use of, are borrowed from the State of natural Bodies, and from thence metaphorically transferred to political Constitutions, one Thing is taken for granted in this Argument, to which I cannot readily assent. It is taken for granted, that as all Animals, by having the Seeds of Decay within themselves, must die sooner or later, therefore political or commercial Institutions are subject to the like Fate, and on the same Principles. Now this remains to be proved; for the Parallel doth not hold in all Respects; and tho' it be true that the Body Politic *may* come to an End, as well as the Body Natural, there is no physical Necessity that it *must*. A Set of Rules and Regulations may be formed for the distributing Property, [the securing and diffusing Industry, the preventing the present shocking Vices of Electioneering, and in general, for the correcting most, if not all of those Evils, which great Riches, Excess of Liberty, and Length of Time, are too apt to introduce. I say such a Set of Rules and Regulations may be formed; against the Admission of which into our Code of Laws, there cannot be the least Pretence of a *Physical Impossibility*. In one Word, the Constitution of the Body Natural is so framed, that after a certain length of Time, no Remedy in Nature can restore it to its pristine Health and Vigour; for at last old Age will necessarily destroy it, if nothing else shall put a Period to it sooner:—But the Diseases of the Body Politic are not *absolutely incurable;* because Care and Caution, and proper Remedies, judiciously and honestly applied, will produce those Effects in one Case, which it would be impossible for them to produce in the other.

INDEX

INDEX